THE PSYCH...
COMEDY

What makes us laugh? Why is comedy so important? How does comedy affect our behaviour?

The Psychology of Comedy provides a unique insight into the role of laughter and humour in our lives. From the mechanics of comedy and what makes a good joke to the health benefits of laughter, the book delves into different types of comedy, from slapstick to complex puns, and the physiological response it provokes. The dark side of comedy is also considered, confronting the idea that what is funny to some can be offensive to others, making this universal experience also highly subjective.

In a time when comedy continues to be one of the most popular and enduring forms of art, *The Psychology of Comedy* reminds us that laughter really is good for the soul.

G. Neil Martin is Honorary Professor of Psychology and former head of department at Regent's University of London, a Life Fellow of the Royal Society of Arts, former books editor of Deadpan magazine and editorial board member of the Annals of Improbable Research.

THE PSYCHOLOGY OF EVERYTHING

People are fascinated by psychology, and what makes humans tick. Why do we think and behave the way we do? We've all met armchair psychologists claiming to have the answers, and people that ask if psychologists can tell what they're thinking. *The Psychology of Everything* is a series of books which debunk the popular myths and pseudo-science surrounding some of life's biggest questions.

The series explores the hidden psychological factors that drive us, from our subconscious desires and aversions, to our natural social instincts. Absorbing, informative, and always intriguing, each book is written by an expert in the field, examining how research-based knowledge compares with popular wisdom, and showing how psychology can truly enrich our understanding of modern life.

Applying a psychological lens to an array of topics and contemporary concerns – from sex, to fashion, to conspiracy theories – *The Psychology of Everything* will make you look at everything in a new way.

Titles in the series:

For further information about this series please visit
www.routledgetextbooks.com/textbooks/thepsychologyofeverything/

THE PSYCHOLOGY OF COMEDY

G. NEIL MARTIN

Routledge
Taylor & Francis Group

LONDON AND NEW YORK

First published 2022
by Routledge
2 Park Square, Milton Park, Abingdon, Oxon OX14 4RN

and by Routledge
605 Third Avenue, New York, NY 10158

Routledge is an imprint of the Taylor & Francis Group, an informa business

British Library Cataloguing-in-Publication Data
A catalogue record for this book is available from the British Library

Library of Congress Cataloging-in-Publication Data
A catalog record for this book has been requested

ISBN: 978-0-367-36610-0 (hbk)
ISBN: 978-0-367-36609-4 (pbk)
ISBN: 978-0-429-34726-9 (ebk)

DOI: 10.4324/9780429347269

Typeset in Joanna
by Apex CoVantage, LLC

Printed and bound by CPI Group (UK) Ltd, Croydon, CR0 4YY

**For Pat and Sharon,
who do like a good laugh**

CONTENTS

PREFACE (THE WARM-UP)

Welcome to a book which some people think should probably not be written: a book on the psychology of comedy.

The reason for this admittedly rocky start is that attempts at understanding comedy, humour and laughter – how comedy "works" – have been condemned as a futile exercise akin to dissecting a frog. This was E.B. White's now famous view from *The Saturday Review of Literature* in 1941.

White argued that while this might be a nice idea, dissecting a frog is likely to kill it and that probably is not a good thing. If you dissect humour, the same outcome follows. "The innards," he continued merrily, "are discouraging to any but the pure scientific mind" [that's probably us] "It won't withstand much poking. It has a certain fragility, an evasiveness which one had best respect." As if to reinforce the point, there is even a book of interviews with humourists called *Poking a Dead Frog*. Bear with me, though. The news does get better. And this book is all about poking.

Batrachian vivisection aside, there is a sizeable body of research not just on humour and comedy but also on why we laugh and smile; on our sense of humour; individual differences in humour production and appreciation; the biology and neurobiology of our response to comedy; the influence of humour on teaching, thinking, memory, advertising, marketing, work, social relations, romantic relations and mental health; and cultural differences in sense of humour and in comedy. Of course, this is different from what White meant – that there is no formula, scientific or otherwise, that can produce the perfect or template comedy, although some comedians and some comedy scriptwriters have tried. The omphalos of his point is that by intervening too surgically and divisively, you will lose some of the magic of comedy because you've killed the thing you want to understand. Comedy is an organic process, driven by serendipity, the muse, creativity, necessity, cleverness, desperation and other unpinable abstractions. How can you predict all of that? Well, some have tried, and some of these attempts are described in this book.

Comedy is one of the most popular art forms in the world. *Roseanne* and *The Big Bang Theory* were ranked in 1st and 2nd place in the most recent US Nielsen TV ratings; four of the most watched programmes of all time in the UK are comedies, including *Only Fools and Horses* (24.35 million viewers in December 1996), *To the Manor Born* (23.95 million viewers in 1979) and *The Benny Hill Show* (21.67 million viewers in 1971). In what seemed like a golden year for comedy, in 1978/9 9 of the top 10 most watched shows in the United States were comedies. The 11th most watched television programme of all time in the United States is a comedy (*M*A*S*H*; 105.9 million viewers), and *M*A*S*H* holds the record for the greatest audience for a season television finale – the 135-minute, 256th episode broadcast on February 28, 1983. Comedy is the fourth most successful film genre in terms of worldwide box office takings, accounting for 14.6% of revenue from 1995 to 2020 (www.the-numbers.com/market/genres). The Royal Institution's 2017 Christmas Lecture featured the science of comedy as its subject, presented by a psychologist. And speaking of Christmas, the Morecambe and Wise Christmas special of 1977 drew an estimated audience of 28,835,000. Two of the most performed Shakespeare plays are his comedies (*A Midsummer Night's Dream* is number 1; *Twelfth Night* is at number 3; there are four others in the top 10: https://priceonomics.com/what-is-shakespeares-most-popular-play/). In short, we like comedy.

Some academics do, too. Two well-established peer-reviewed journals are devoted exclusively to comedy and humour: *Humor: The International Journal of Humor Research* (published by De Gruyter) and *Comedy Studies* (published by Taylor & Francis). The former is supported by an international society which hosts major international conferences. Two new online journals of humour have recently appeared: the *European Journal of Humour Research* and the *Israeli Journal of Humor*. There is a vibrant market for books about humour and comedy, including comedian autobiographies (passim); trade books such as Alan Zweibel's *Laugh Lines* (Abrams Press, 2020), Jimmy Carr and Lucy Graves's *The Naked Jape* (2006, Michael Joseph) and *Only Joking* (2006, Gotham Books), Kliph Nesteroff's *The Comedians* (Grove Press, 2016), Robert Provine's *Curious Behaviour* (2014, Harvard University Press) and *Laughter* (2001, Penguin), Scott Weems's *Ha!* (2014, Basic Books), Stephanie Davies's *Laughology* (2013, Crown Horse Publishing), Peter McGraw and Joel Warner's *The Humor Code* (2014, Simon & Schuster), Jonathan Lynn's *Comedy Rules* (2012, Faber & Faber) and Oxford University Press's short introductions to *Comedy* and *Humour*; books about comedies such as *The Office*, *The League of Gentlemen*, *Curb Your Enthusiasm*, *Saturday Night Live* and *Rising Damp*; and more academic texts such as Rod Martin and Thomas Ford's *The Psychology of Humour* (2018, Academic Press), Janet Gibson's *An Introduction to the Psychology of Humour* (2019, Routledge) and Matthew Hurley et al.'s *Inside Jokes* (2013, MIT Press).

What draws a scientist to this particular bailiwick of intellectual inquiry rather than mindfulness, social priming or parallel-distributed processing (please feel free to skip this part and go to p. xviii, if mildly self-indulgent and self-effacing autobiography is not your thing)? Like many lovers of comedy, I was one of those people who would tape comedy shows from the radio and television. Mike Schur, one of the writers and producers on the United States *The Office*, used to tape *The David Letterman Show*, write down the jokes and stories and tell them to his friends in school the next day. Judd Apatow, Amy Schumer, Garry Shandling, Jerry Seinfeld and others used to record *Saturday Night Live* off the television, because there was nothing quite like it at the time.

Recording in the days before the glamour of video, I spooled 30-minute comedies meticulously onto a 90-minute Memorex or a BASF audio tape cassette (long play to squeeze the tape time), with these names – like St Ivel, Unigate, St Michael and Woolworths – time-locked to certain type of childhood. Proustian magneto-ferrous memories. Evening recordings graduated to mesonoxian cataloguing with late night comedy and variety shows such as Brian Matthews's *Around Midnight, Steve Madden*, and other matutinal sounds finding their place in the library. At one stage, I was invited onto one of these shows – Jeremy Beadle's late-night show on BBC Radio 2 – because of something I had written and sent in. Once the interview was finished, the producer asked if I would be interested in submitting material to future shows. I was thrilled. I submitted some jokes to *Steve Wright in the Afternoon* when it was on BBC Radio 1, and it broadcast my first joke on national radio. I won a bottle of champagne on HTV's *All Kinds of Everything* for phoning in an entry for its graffiti wall. Inspired by *Giles Brandreth's Book of Fascinating Facts*, I started writing a column for a Welsh-language local newspaper, *Papur Y Cwm*, terrorising the good burghers of South West Wales with gobbets of obscure information such as the length of time it takes to boil an ostrich's egg (40 minutes), still the one fact I remember ineluctably from that time. I wrote *Neil's News Weekly* at primary school – essentially stuff filched, re-packaged or inspired by *TV Times* and the slew of IPC comics (*Cheeky, Krazy, Buster, Whizzer and Chips, Monster Fun*, the whole library). "Weekly" was a tad ambitious. It became Fortnightly, then Monthly. Never Annually. The headmaster offered me a pristine sheaf of beige, silky, lined foolscap to work on, as the nearest most of us really got to creativity was making deformed animals out of plasticine and lanterns out of toxic paint at Christmas. It was too nice to scribble on, and I think I saved it for something else.

I started collecting comedy records and tapes and listening to them endlessly. My Methuen library was enormous. There was *The Good Bok* and the massive *Life of Brian* book and the *NOT!s* and *Auberon Waugh's Private Eye Diaries* and the Stephen Piles and *The Young Ones* and *The Two Ronnies* joke books and Roger Wilmut's *From Fringe to Flying Circus* . . .

and . . . well every other staple of printed comedy at that time. I did routines from Dave Allen – I wrote down some of the best jokes in my book to entertain (that was the ambition) family and visitors. I used to be able to quote "The News in Welsh" sketch from *I'm Sorry I'll Read That Again* in full (from a magnificent LP called *"We Are Most Amused"*) and remember quite a tranche of the *Kinda Lingers* double LP; I later snuck the last song of the final series of *Not the Nine O'Clock News* into a hyperlink in my work email signature 30 years later just before I left that particular institution. No one noticed. Don't tell anyone. I was obsessed with who wrote what for which comedy shows, especially sketch shows. They became idols: names like Colin Bostock-Smith, Neil Shand, Tony Sarchet, Kim Fuller, Richard Curtis, Andrea Solomons and others.

I submitted (in retrospect, rather dire) sketches to television comedy shows that were topical. One particularly dreadful example was sent to *Carrott's Lib*, a live, satirical BBC 1 show broadcast on Saturday night, and I received the typical, and entirely justified, rejection letter from the producer. I told this story at the British Film Institute in London to the same producer who wrote that rejection letter (Geoff Posner, for it was he). He was very nice about it. But he was right. It was a terrible sketch. Geoff is right about everything. I remember it now. And I am still too traumatised to tell you about it. *Carrott's Lib* also featured one of the most perfect sketches about idiocy ever written, breath-taking in its cleverness and silliness (it involves an outfit called The Sun Readers' Liberation Army and you can find it here: www. youtube.com/watch?v=OO687AiGIvU). By another twist of fate, in 2014, I ended up working at the same university as one of the show's (and many other shows') writers. David Hanson is a kind, warm and generous man who even tolerated listening to a two-hour lecture on the psychology of comedy by me. In it, I use a clip from Larry David's *Curb Your Enthusiasm* which features the gratuitous but brilliant use of a particular swear word (described in Chapter 1). David came up to me afterwards and said, as if he was telling me about his breakfast cereal, that he once worked with Larry David. He also created Max Headroom.

This started a bug, and I started writing off to all other sketch shows I thought might be interested in my slightly more competently crafted sketches and quickies . . . *Naked Radio, A Kick Up the Eighties, Spitting Image*. I was placed on some writers register (not as sinister then as it sounds now) and so I received letters from producers requesting submissions to shows such as *Laugh, I Nearly Paid My Licence Fee* (look it up, it's not great and the invitation letter was funnier than the show, but it starred Robbie Coltrane) and, of course, *Spitting Image*. I still have the sweet letter of feedback sent to me from John Lloyd, and I did suggest that David Owen and David Steel share a bed together a la Morecambe and Wise.

As this was going on, my sixth form friend, Charles Williams, and I thought it would be a hoot to write a satirical magazine about the worlds of politics, entertainment and Tregib County Secondary School for the captive Llandeilo school market. We called it F***!, and we printed about 50 copies (from memory, the biology lab technician helped; I left this to Charles — it was probably blackmail). We might have got away with the worlds of politics and entertainment but the headmaster and the board of governors had different ideas about Tregib County Secondary School. After one week's suspension, a formal summons before the board of governors, a further week's suspension for not being contrite enough in front of the board of governors and for publishing a tongue-in cheek apology which compounded our original crimes and an apology to all staff and pupils we wrote about, we were allowed back in. The magazine was called *Frog!* That's what we said. The cover is reproduced here.

Charles wrote about the episode, brilliantly, in his then newspaper *The Western Mail*, and the article is well worth seeking out, if only for the deft use of the word "cobwebby". You can find him on Twitter as @charleswms.

My undergraduate research project was focused on comedy (you'll read more about it in Chapter 1), and I turned my mind to what I could do after graduation. I'd written a spoof of *The Independent*'s very famous and photographically ground-breaking *Magazine* and sent it off to *Private Eye* and asked if it was looking for a writer. At the time,

Hartlepool had received a lot of attention in the paper for being a town full of drunks, and the spoof magazine used this as a hook for the content. I called it *The Indepubsagain Magazine*, and I'm still proud of some of the things I wrote in it.

The recordings continued – *The Mary Whitehouse Experience*, *Victor Lewis-Smith*, *Son of Cliché* . . . I applied for and got a PhD studentship to study chemoreception at the University of Warwick, after having turned down the opportunity to be a local reporter for *The South Wales Guardian*. At around that time, I also went for an interview for a reporter job at *The Doctor Magazine*, based in a cramped, second-floor office somewhere in Guildford where everyone seemed very angry (I flunked that interview), and I wrote to the BBC to ask for one of its Trainee Comedy Producer application forms.

After I'd accepted the Warwick offer and moved to Leamington Spa, I got a call from the *Private Eye* office one afternoon. I wasn't in. Too late. I had committed to academia. But I reasoned that I could write and do the PhD. The other way around would be too awkward and impractical. I published the undergraduate comedy study about a year later.

In 1994, a new magazine about comedy – let's be honest, the only magazine about comedy – was launched in the UK. Edited by a man so good they named him twice (David Davies, who later edited *Q Magazine*), *Deadpan* was a mix of interviews, features, reviews, listings and jokes. Anyone who was anyone in mid-1990s comedy was in there. Stewart Lee and Barry Took had a column. I sent in a piece about the 50 Most Irritating Modern Things –something like that. The editor liked it and commissioned me to write some comedians' gig reviews for the magazine. The first was of Charlie Chuck. In Leicester. I still accepted the second commission. From there, I became the magazine's books editor until the magazine folded around two years later. I was very proud to be part of *Deadpan* and, through it, got to meet Rob Newman and Phil Jupitus. I could also boast that I had a column next to Stewart Lee. Until no-one wanted a magazine about comedy anymore.

And that is where this all started.

The book is called *The Psychology of Comedy*, rather than *The Psychology of Humour*, and there are two reasons for this. First, there is another fine book called *The Psychology of Humor* written by another Martin, and two books by a person with the same surname would probably be too much for most people. Second, and less facetiously, this is a book about humour and comedy more broadly. It reviews a large body of research on humour itself but also includes theories of humour and comedy, as well as so-called humour styles, lavishly illustrated by examples from literature, TV, radio, film and stand-up comedy.

The first chapter takes you through definitions of comedy, humour and "sense of humour" and examines what makes a joke a joke. It describes the circumstances under which smiling and laughter are produced and reviews the evidence that humour styles exist. The second chapter reviews some of the theories of humour of comedy and laughter – historical and contemporary. The third chapter takes us into the territory of the personal and the individual differences which affect our response to comedy – our sex, our culture and our personality. The personality theme continues in Chapter 4 where research on comedians' and other performers' personalities is described and reviewed. Comedy and humour is also used to make people laugh and smile in a more instructional, directed way, and Chapter 5 looks at the uses of humour and comedy in health, in psychotherapy and in causing offence. The partner chapter, number 6, examines how humour and comedy have been used in education, marketing and advertising. Finally, the last chapter examines the role of physiology and neuropsychology in our understanding of comedy.

Comedy is perennial but it morphs and sifts and slithers proteanly depending on the time, the mores and the attitudes of those that consume it. Some comedy considered socially pleasurable 40 years ago might seem ripe to the modern eye and ear. While I was writing the final chapter of this book, comedy again was in the news. UKTV Gold had withdrawn "The Germans" episode of Fawlty Towers for the use of two specific, race-related words; The Mighty Boosh, Come Fly With Me and Little Britain had their shows removed from some streaming services because of their use of "blackface". To further illustrate this intersection, the black British comedian and academic, Lenny Henry, interviewed by Louis Theroux for a COVID lockdown interview on BBC Radio 4 just two weeks before George Floyd's death, recounted that, even now, after his success and despite being undeniably recognisable, he continues to be racially abused on the tube. His autobiography, *Who Am I, Again?*, describes the beginnings of his career in comedy as a black man. In what is a complex area fraught with potential offence (Henry was famously part of the *Black and White Minstrel* BBC TV music show in which people would "black up"), his Hollywood debut in 1991, *True Identity*, featured a black character pretending to be a white man. The comedy of offence is considered in Chapter 1.

When I started work on the book, I asked various chums and visitors to my Twitter page to send me their favourite for the book. I want to thank all of them here: @roystoncartoons, @vincegraff, @emilynordmann, @tonyhusband1, @coulls, @mimisparkler, @jennirodd, @at_doherty, @drsfink, @dbirwinIII, @philosophic_lee, @joonloons, @hetha2009, @drkimble123 and @lapsusLima. Thanks also to Dr Niki Daniel and Dr Nicky Brunswick for reading every line of the draft and giving me punctilious feedback and comments; to Kiersten and Daniel, for being such good and well-behaved little people; Kasha Patel from NASA for allowing me to burble some early thoughts about what is in here (Kasha is also a stand-up; you can find her on Twitter: @KashaPatel); Cri Cuomo for her thoughts on an early chapter; everyone at Routledge/Taylor & Francis involved in the production of the book; and Ceri McLardy for commissioning a book that wasn't meant to happen (that's a story for a different time, and since Ceri commissioned the book, she's given birth – hurrah!). Finally, an enormous thanks to David Quantick, Joel Morris, Professor Richard Wiseman and Phil Hughes who went beyond the call of duty and read the final version and provided the comments they did for the book. Genuinely, thank you.

The book was written right in the middle of COVID-19. One of the few benefits of a pandemic is that it makes you write and deliver your book more quickly. And here it is. I do hope you'll enjoy it. If you do, please let me know (Twitter: @thatneilmartin; email: NeilOnComedy@outlook.com). And it you want a copy of F***!, it's yours for 50 pounds.

1

AN INTRODUCTION TO THE PSYCHOLOGY OF COMEDY

THE QUEST FOR THE WORLD'S FUNNIEST JOKE

In 2001, Richard Wiseman, a psychologist at the University of Hertfordshire, set out on a quest: to find the world's funniest joke.

The quest was no joke.

As part of the British Association for the Advancement of Science's Festival of Science, Dr Wiseman and his colleagues asked the public to send in their funniest jokes and people would rate them online, via a site called The Laugh Lab. They received 500 jokes in the first 24 hours. The site received over 300,000 visitors.

Visitors rated each of the jokes on a five-point scale, from not very funny to very funny, and after data collection had ended, the team calculated the results and identified the joke rated the least funny and the funniest. The average length of the jokes submitted was 40 words; the funniest contained 103 words. If jokes were rude or offensive, they were excluded from the study.

The worst joke was this:

"Why did the chicken cross the road?"
"To get to the other side."

It is one you'll be very familiar with, and you'll probably not disagree with the judgement.

DOI: 10.4324/9780429347269-1

The most frequently submitted joke – submitted 300 times – was "What's brown and sticky? A stick". Hardly anyone found it funny.

The research team also examined the most popular/funniest type of joke within a class of joke, such as doctor jokes or "idiot" jokes – those that derive their humour from disparaging a specific group of people, whether by sex, nationality, hair colour, region and so on – and surreal jokes such as "What do you do with a wombat?" ("Play wom").

But the best joke was submitted by a Geoff Anandappa from Blackpool. Here it is, in full.

Sherlock Holmes and Dr Watson were going camping. They pitched their tent under the stars and went to sleep. Sometime in the middle of the night Holmes woke Watson up and said: "Watson, look up at the stars, and tell me what you see."

Watson replied: "I see millions and millions of stars."

Holmes said: "And what do you deduce from that?"

Watson replied: "Well, if there are millions of stars, and if even a few of those have planets, it's quite likely there are some planets like earth out there. And if there are a few planets like Earth out there, there might also be life."

And Holmes said: "Watson, you idiot, it means that somebody stole our tent."

Your marks out of 10?

DEFINING HUMOUR AND COMEDY

Research in comedy and humour is beset with problems of taxonomy and definition. Psychology's interest in both began, in earnest, in 1972 with Goldstein and McGhee's book, *The Psychology of Humour: Theoretical Perspectives and Empirical Issues.* The first international conference on humour and laughter was held in Cardiff in 1976. But this was a long time coming. Psychology up until the 1970s had occupied itself with the study of misery rather than joy, exhibiting what Allport (1960) called the "tenderness taboo". A study of 172 introductory psychology textbooks published between 1877 and 1961 found that two to three times more space was devoted to the understanding of negative emotion than positive (Carlson, 1966). Of course, all of this has changed now, and psychologists fall over themselves to study all types of positive emotions. But humour tends to get short shrift in textbooks – in one study, only 3 out of 136 introductory psychology texts referred to humour, and those 3 were published before 1930 (Roeckelein, 2002). It is at least moderately reassuring that some modern ones are trying to correct this terrible omission (Martin & Carlson, 2018).

There are broad definitions of humour and comedy – and discussions regarding whether there is a distinction between them, generally concluding that there is – and there are definitions of certain types of comedy. Literally, "humour" derives from the Latin for "fluid" or "liquid" (humorem), and the Greek physician Hippocrates considered that our health depended on a balance of four of these fluids or humours: blood, phlegm, black bile and yellow bile. Another physician with just as significant an effect on the history of psychology, Galen, argued that imbalance in the humours would lead to the expression of specific psychological characteristics – you might be regarded as phlegmatic or sanguine, for example.

Humour and laughter are mutually exclusive – you can have one without the other – you can laugh at things that are not funny and you can find material funny but not laugh. In fact, until around the 16th century humour was barely ever connected with laughter or mirth. At that point, it had a very different meaning from the one we use today. Then, it was considered a deviation from social norms, reflecting someone who was an oddball or an eccentric (Martin, 2006). The 18th century marked the era when humour took on more positive connotations, with people admiring and enjoying those who amused others. The 18th century also saw the word ridicule (from Latin ridiculum, meaning joke) becoming common currency and used to refer to anything that caused laughter, although its use was seen as aggressive (this is the way we use it today). And this is where we can get stuck in the weeds of etymology because the word wit begins to be used where ridicule applied. Wit was seen as a verbally aggressive, acidic form of humour and a sign of the user's cleverness and linguistic dexterity: more aristocratic. Humour was considered to be a more benign, humanitarian way of amusing others: more bourgeois. The word "humourist" emerged as the mot juste for a person who wrote funny things in the mid-19th century.

According to the Oxford English Dictionary, humour is defined as "quality of action, speech or writing which excited amusement, oddity, jocularity, facetiousness, comicality, fun" and "the faculty of perceiving what is ludicrous or amusing or expressing it in speech, writing or other composition". The Cambridge English Dictionary, as many other dictionaries do, defines comedy in terms of genre, as "a (type of) film, play or book that is intentionally funny either in its characters or its actions".

All definitions of comedy refer to the source of the humour – whether it is a film, play or literary work – with secondary definitions encompassing its reference to the amusement in situations or to humour styles. Martin's (2006) fairly comprehensive definition of humour is "anything that people say or do that is perceived as funny and tends to make others laugh, as well as the mental processes that go into both creating and perceiving such an amusing stimulus, and also the affective response involved in the enjoyment of it". This more or less covers stimulus, response and disposition. Martin argues that the humour process comprises four components: social context, cognitive-perceptual processes, emotional response and vocal or behavioural expression of laughter. He describes humour as being "fundamentally a social phenomenon", but this not especially true. There is no need for social engagement if you're reading a funny book or watching a funny exchange when you're out in public or if you're watching a funny show on Netflix or if you're enjoying the latest influencer's make-up nightmare on YouTube. But it is true in the sense that it forms part of our social interaction, and an important one; it allows us to engage with each other paratelically. Apter (1991) had put forward the proposition that we have two states of mind, one of which predisposes us to joke, use humour and be playful (the paratelic state). The more sombre and serious state is telic, and we dovetail between the two throughout the course of the day.

Thinkers throughout the ages have held different views about humour and laughter. Humour, according to Darwin (1872), who discussed the subject at length in *The Expression of Emotions in Man and Animals*, was the "tickling of the mind", and he observed laughing and grinning occurred across primate species. He recalls his colleague, a Dr Duchenne (to whom we will return a little later), who kept a tame monkey which when fed delicacies would raise the corners of its mouth as if in a state of pleasant satisfaction (Darwin, 1872).

Plato, on the other hand, was no fan of humour or laughter. "When we laugh at our friends' ridiculous conditions," wrote Plato, "logic declares we mix pleasure with envy and blend, therefore, pleasure and pain." In *Philebus* he makes an aggressive case for the prosecution, arguing that the sense of the ridiculous is based on a lack of self-knowledge. Laughter, in this context, is malevolent, arising from aggression or spite and a wish to see your enemy bested. Similar sentiments were expressed by Cicero and Quintilian, both of whom regarded humour and laughter as the most pas of social faux pas and more – corrupting morals, art and religion. Mind you, the Bible wasn't overly keen either. Of all the references to laughter (29 of them) in the angry, arid termagant that is the Old Testament, most are in the context of mocking others or are reflections of contempt (Koestler, 1964).

Freud, as you might expect, also had a lot to say on the topic and wrote a treatise on the nature of jokes (see the next chapter). Freud (1960) viewed humour as a means of coping with distress: it was "the loftiest of the mechanisms available to [humans] for the adaptation to suffering", a sentiment also echoed by Nabokov in *Strong Opinions*, where he argued that "a good laugh is the best pesticide" (we'll come to the use of humour as a detoxifier – or toxifer – later). Alan Ayckbourn, too, was at one with Freud, believing that "comedy is tragedy interrupted". Many of these views see comedy as a balm or an antiseptic to ameliorate something toxic or gangrenous. Max Beerbohm put it more starkly: "Humour undiluted is the most depressing of all phenomena. Humour must have its background of seriousness. Without this context there comes none of that incongruity which is the mainspring of laughter." It's unclear whether that makes humour depressing or how it works best, but we'll return to this notion of incongruity in the next chapter. It is the bedrock of a major theory of humour.

The types of humour and comedy are many. Speck (1991) identified five of them: comic wit, satire, sentimental comedy, sentimental humour and full comedy. Kelly and Solomon (1975) identified seven humour categories: puns, understatement, jokes, something ludicrous, satire, irony and intent. Others have created different typologies. Buijzen and Valkenburg (2004) proposed slapstick, clownish, surprise, misunderstanding, irony, satire and parody. Sometimes humour research is the right place to be if you want an argument. In one of the more famous studies of humour taxonomy, Long and Graesser (1988) examined people's conversations and monitored the types of humour used within them. Participants were more likely to laugh and attempt humour if they were with others (a point we'll explore in more detail later). These were no ordinary conversations, but exchanges between participants (guest and host) on television shows such as the US *The Tonight Show*. Based on this exercise, they identified 11 categories of humour that participants use in interactions:

1 irony
2 satire
3 sarcasm
4 over and understatement
5 self-deprecation
6 teasing
7 replies to rhetorical questions
8 clever replies to serious statements

9 double entendres
10 transforming expressions into new statements
11 puns

There are "humorous" phrases that we use that may not be especially funny but signal that something funny is being said – stock phrases that are trite. "As the actress said to the bishop" is one example which follows a statement that could have a lubricious or innocent meaning. An example relentlessly used in the US version of The Office by Michael Scott was "that's what she said" which serves a similar function.

Sometimes humour is unintentional – there may be a slip of the tongue, or a physical faux pas is committed or some physical corporeal act is committed that is incongruous and is, therefore, funny. You've Been Framed, the clip show full of serendipitous gaucheness, trades off our love of these well. Verbal humour might include puns but also unintentional lapses such as malapropisms (using a word that is similar in sound to the one you want but has a totally different meaning) and Spoonerisms where the first letters of words are transposed. A deliberate working of this is seen in the name of The Kenny Everett Television Show's dragged-up, feather-boaed Hollywood starlet, Cupid Stunt.

A reasonable question to ask is: given how common and ubiquitous comedy and laughter are, what are their purpose? What function do they serve? Some, such as Fry (1987), have argued that laughter makes no sense in evolutionary terms because we are expending energy unnecessarily. Other views hold that humour has evolved to promote social bonding, facilitate co-operation, prevent pursuing counter-productive initiatives, signal non-threatening behaviour, to signal a desire to initiate or maintain social cooperation, manipulate status, resolve errors in a positive way, attract a mate, or signal an awareness that the user shares similar attitudes and preferences to those they are interacting with So, let's consider one of the most basic, cognitive forms of humour and comedy: the joke.

WHAT IS A JOKE?

A joke is one of the most complex pieces of linguistic content we can exchange with another human being. It is subject to a number of cognitive, cultural and social constraints, but particularly cognitive ones. Jokes demand cognitive machinery, and if this machinery is absent or malfunctioning or not well-greased, jokes don't work. Sometimes viewed as the psychological evolution of physical stimulation – one theory of laughter proposes that tickling and humour share the same origin where the older, physical form (tickling) has been replaced by a more psychological form (the use of humour) – a joke itself requires (1) an understanding of syntax and content, (2) the maintenance of information in mind as the joke progresses because the punchline will depend on the previous material being remembered and (3) domain-specific knowledge (the joke's content). According to Freud (1960) "there are only two purposes that it [a joke] may serve. It is either a hostile joke or an obscene joke", a bicameralism that we will see is not entirely justified.

Primitive attempts at humour are attempts at slapstick, where mirth or joy is derived from the perception of physical acts. And we do still derive enjoyment from this type of comedy – it is one of the most successful exports across cultures because it does not rely on the knowledge and understanding of language. We will come back to this type of comedy in the section on culture in Chapter 3, but it is widespread and well consumed – from the films of Laurel and Hardy; the physical humour of Harpo Marx, Buster Keaton, Charlie Chaplin and clowns in general; to later comedians and actors who rely on movement and non-verbal material to make people laugh. One sketch, a non-verbal one, from *Not the Nine O'Clock News* features Rowan Atkinson as a fey pedestrian walking along a pavement who spots a camera filming him. He shyly waves and carries on walking until his distraction leads him to bump into a lamp post. This is immediately followed by a similar scenario where he is again walking, spots the camera but this time, as he is about to bump into another lamp post, notices it in time, turns to the camera satisfied by his pre-emption, walks on and falls down a pub's open cellar door.

Jokes often require us to place ourselves in the positions of others or to understand others' intentions – a process known as mentalising. Dunbar, Marriott and Duncan (1997) found that around two-thirds of natural conversations involve us undertaking mentalising of this sort because we are engaged in understanding the social behaviour of others and how and why they behave. Dunbar also points out an interesting observation about the limits of our mentalising. He and his co-researchers found that in Shakespeare's plays and two genres of film, these contained scenes including speaking parts that did not exceed the number of people we can engage in conversation with (Krems & Dunbar, 2013; Dezecache & Dunbar, 2012). There seems to be a natural limit to our mentalising, and Dunbar, Launay and Curry (2016) have argued that complex verbal humour which out-wits, stretches or exhausts this mentalising will not work: people won't understand it. "Jokes should not exceed the mentalizing competences of the audience," they caution, sagely.

Some of the best examples of the complexity of jokes is found in puns, and puns trade on lexical ambiguity, as illustrated by Douglas Copeland's *Worst. Person. Ever* in which a character remarks, "The fucker was singing eighties pop tunes in the key of hepatitis C". In linguistics, there are a number of identifiable forms of lexical ambiguity, and a lot of them revolve around sounds and spellings. Rodd, Gilbert and Betts (2017) cite a study in which over 80% of common words in English had more than one dictionary entry or definition. One of the earliest facts I remember from my childhood is that the word "set" has over 46 different meanings (it's a great homonym). Homographs describe words that are identically spelled but are phonetically different – "sow" and "close" are two good examples. Homophones are words that may be differently spelled but are phonetically identical – "bear" and "bare", for example, which means that to understand these in speech, you need the context in which they appear. Psycholinguists argue that we process words automatically and their different meanings quickly and in parallel (in milliseconds) before we decide on which word makes the best fit (they call this the "exhaustive access model").

Here's one very good example of lexical ambiguity and a pun. It is from the radio presenter and comedian, Jon Holmes. Commenting on David and Victoria Beckham's lavish, if extravagant and (to some) vulgar, furnishing arrangements for their wedding venue, he issued the following majestic reproof:

"People in crass houses should not stow thrones"

which is not only the best pun ever created but is highly complex. The overall pun involves the understanding and knowledge of a specific proverb ("People in glass houses . . ." etc), the understanding of the individuals involved, an understanding of specific items, an understanding of specific contexts and venues, then a specific pun ("crass"/"glass"), then the piece de resistance – a deliberate Spoonerism which juxtaposes the first and second parts of the words to form the pun on "throw stones". It is unimprovable.

A similar complexity can be found in comedian Tim Robbins's warm-up joke, which goes something like this. A Frenchman and an Englishman are having a bet on whose cat can swim the channel fastest. The English cat is called: "One Two Three", the French one is called "Un Deux Trois." Which one won? The English one because Un Deux Trois Quatre Cinq. (sound it out: "Un Deux Trois cat sank")

Here are a couple more examples, this time from Tim Vine:

"Maladies, maladies, maladies, maladies . . . but that's enough of the formalities."

"A man walks into a butcher's. He said: 'I'll bet you £10 you can't reach those steaks hanging up there!' The butcher says, 'I'm sorry, but the stakes are too high!' "

The pun being, of course, on steak/stake and a reliance on the understanding of betting and the understanding of butchers' shops.

Here's another relatively complex pun, from @ItsAndyRyan on Twitter:

Me: Is there any particular way you don't want your name pronounced?

Percy: Not per se

And here is Jimmy Carr's clever joke, based on semantics:

"Throwing acid is wrong. In some people's eyes."

While we think of jokes as unitary, often, of course, they aren't. There are riddles, knock-knock jokes and doctor-doctor jokes that follow a fairly rigid format. Some even have specialised names. One joke, named after the prolific British comedy scriptwriter John Langdon, involves taking the listener down a garden path and surprising him or her at the end. It's illustrated when you have a joke involving two characters and the description of who you think is of one (the obvious one) turns out to be the description of the other. A good example of this can be found in the second series of *I'm Alan Partridge* where Norfolk Nights disk jockey, Alan Partridge, is organising a day's whole viewing of the James Bond canon on video in his static caravan but has promised to drive his PA, Lynn, to her mother's grave. Here's the exchange with the day's organiser, Alan's girlfriend Sonja:

Sonja: Can we finish writing the Bond schedule?

Lynn: Oh, you've made allowances for the visit to my mother's grave?

Alan: Yes, that's in the schedule. Visit to your mother's grave, then Dr. No. The underground base of an evil genius . . . and then Dr. No!

The Langdon is the last line, where the subject is inverted. One of my favourite sketches, written by Neil MacVicar, from *Not the Nine O'Clock News* misleads you into thinking that a nervous young English man, Adrian, and a seasoned, older Russian man, Ivan, are meeting in some woods to discuss the former's recruitment as a Russian spy. The joke, however, is that the Russian has very different intentions. After an exchange of information, it ends:

> **Ivan**: Good. Then we leave for Moscow tonight.
> **Adrian**: Wonderful. I'll think I'll be the best spy you've ever had!
> **Ivan**: Spy? Spy?!!! [snorts]. No boyfriend of mine goes out to work. . .

When General Pinochet visited Margaret Thatcher in the UK in the 1980s, the *Veep* and *The Life and Times of David Copperfield* scriptwriter, Simon Blackwell, said that the weekly satirical BBC Radio 4 show, *Weekending*, was "shitting Langdons". It's a popular type of joke and crops up in many familiar places.

What are the funniest words?

Everyone seems to have a funny word or a word that sets them off – it could sound funny or it could have some personal significance. In another *Not the Nine O'Clock News* sketch, Gerald the Gorilla, a professor, is interviewed with a great ape he is thought to have cultivated, but the ape turns out to be more ineffably middle class and urbane than he is. Gerald corrects the professor's misuse of collective nouns saying, "It's a *whoop* of gorillas, Professor; it's a *flange* of baboons". Flange is a favourite word that has entered the comedy lexicon. It's a nice, funny word, fricative then labio-dental. It is also, famously, completely made-up. Continuing the NOT theme, Rowan Atkinson's extended pronunciation of the word "Bob" in the *Blackadder* TV sitcom is another that people find funny although the word lacks any intrinsic humorous merit.

Creating a taxonomy of funny words is a hard job but somebody has attempted to undertake it. Tomas Engelthaler and Thomas T. Hills sought to obtain humour ratings of 4997 English words from 821 participants (Engelthaler & Hills, 2018). The words were taken from previously collected word norms used in studies. There were some predictable responses but also some surprises, especially when the authors looked at differences according to participants' age and sex.

Table 1.1 lists the words listed as most positive and negative in terms of their humorousness and words judged by men and women as being most humorous.

Word which people judge to be the most humorous (these showed the largest differences between men and women)	Words rated by women as most humorous	Words with the most extreme positive humour ratings	Words with the most extreme negative humour ratings
Bondage	Giggle	Booty	Rape
Birthmark	Beast	Tit	Torture
Orgy	Circus	Booby	Torment
Brand	Grand	Hooter	Gunshot
Chauffeur	Juju	Nitwit	Death
Doze	Humbug	Twit	Nightmare
Buzzard	Slicker	Waddle	War
Czar	Sweat	Tinkle	Trauma
Weld	Ennui	Bebop	Rapist
Prod	Holder	Egghead	Distrust
Corn	Momma	Ass	Deathbed
Raccoon	Sod	Twerp	Pain

SMILING AND LAUGHTER

Comedy needs an audience – whether it's one person or thousands – but it also needs a response. Two obvious behavioural responses to comedy and humour are smiling and laughter, and collectively they comprise what is called "mirth". Mirth may range from a Giaconda-style enigmatic smile, to a grin, a chuckle, laughter and helpless convulsion, all of which indicate to others that we are enjoying ourselves. But what is less obvious is that laughter tends not to be generated by humour in day-to-day interactions, but by the more prosaic content and nature of that interaction itself. We laugh at things in conversation that are not objectively funny. It is as if this vocal unguent oils the machinery of social interaction, and there are explanations for this and why we laugh with others even though we think that what they say is not funny. Smiling is also a typical response to a vocal or visual stimulus we find amusing or entertaining, but a smile can have many hidden and overt meanings. Herman Melville (1852) once wrote that a smile "is the chosen vehicle for all ambiguities". So, let's consider whether we can sieve some clarity from these ambiguities.

SMILING

Why do we smile? According to Dale Carnegie, "a smile says, 'I like you. You make me happy. I am glad to see you'". We smile because we are content, we smile when we see or hear something which makes us happy, we smile to make others comfortable with us, we smile when we're embarrassed, we smile when we are actually unhappy, we do so when we want to put people at ease and when we greet others, we smile when we would like others to do something for us or when we would like them to respond positively to a request for help or action, but we also smile when we want to express disapproval or displeasure – Darwin's "derisive smile" – when we might smile sarcastically or threateningly. One study even found that we smile more when we imagine being with someone that we know than when we're alone (Fridlund et al., 1990), while another found that we remember smiling faces better than we do non-smiling ones (Tsuki-ura & Cabeza, 2008). Smiling is also infectious – smiling makes others smile. Spike Milligan wrote about this in his poem, "Smiling," "Smiling is infectious / you catch it like the flu, / When someone smiled at me today, / I started smiling too / So if you feel a smile begin / don't leave it undetected / Let's start an epidemic quick, / and get the world infected!" Safer and nicer than COVID.

People have been found to respond more strongly to smiling eyes than to whole faces or mouths in a study in which activation in the amygdala – a subcortical structure in the brain – was measured when people watched images of facial features (Meletti et al., 2012). This response occurred 300 to 400 ms after the onset of the stimulus – individuals took longer to look at "smiling" features than ones expressing fear (200 to 400ms). Other research has confirmed that smiling has a number of benefits – transgressions are treated more leniently if the transgressor smiles, and displeasure in others is also reduced if we smile at them. People who try to persuade others – to get your vote or to get a potential date with you – smile (LaFrance, Hecht & Paluck, 2003). Some professions mandate it – a trip on an airline is evidence enough of this as soon as you board your plane. Fred Sirieix, former maître d' at Galvin at Windows and seemingly permanent maître d' of the *First Dates* restaurant, insists on implementing the positive mantra he calls the three Ss: See, Smile and Say Hello. The smile masks and expresses a myriad of intentions.

One theory of the evolution of laughter argues that this vocalisation is an extension of smiling, and evolutionary thinkers have debated whether these two behaviours are distinct and different or whether laughter is an intense form of smiling (Lockard, Fahren-bruch, Smith & Morgan, 1977). Another view argues that both were different in non-human primates but converged in humans. Lockard et al. (1977), for example, list a number of primate species in which these two types of expression are different (one characterised by silent teeth-bearing, the other with vocal, open-mouthed behaviour).

Whatever smiling's ontogeny, we do know that smiling is accompanied by specific types of motor activity in the face and that our physiognomy changes depending on the type of smile. For example, much research has focused on the famous Duchenne smile – the so-called genuine smile – as this seems to recruit additional muscle activity to smiling that is not genuine. Two sets of muscles are normally mentioned in this context: the zygomatic major muscles around the corners of the mouth (which are activated in all smiles, as smiling is defined by the upward lifting of the corners of both sides of the mouth) and the orbicular oculi muscles around the eyes which are thought to be activated during genuine expressions of positive affect. It is named after the French anatomist, Duchenne de Boulogne and author of *Mecanisme de la physionomie humaine*. Studies have found, for example, that the former muscles are activated when people are asked to smile, but both are activated when people spontaneously smile (Martin, Rychlowska, Wood, & Niedenthal, 2017). But, as always in psychology, the picture is not this clear-cut. Some evidence suggests that people are able to fake genuine smiles (and when you know what is required to do this, it's not difficult), while other research has found no such activation of oculi muscles when people claim that they're happy, thus questioning its (the Duchenne smile's) ability to distinguish between genuine and false emotional states. Our zygomatic muscles are also activated in situations which are not positive or, at least, which are not specifically associated with happiness, such as embarrassment, misery, pride and greeting other people (Martin et al., 2017).

One way in which smiling has been conceived is that it reflects signals about our intentions and social motives. The Simulation of Smiles Model, for example, suggests that we produce certain types of smiles to service different motivational and behavioural needs. Specifically, they reinforce behaviour that is desirable, they help us form relationships with others or they help us set and preserve social hierarchies (reward, affiliation and dominant smiles, respectively). This is not to say that you can only express one type of intention in a smile; you can express two types of intention in a smile. The important difference in this model –compared to the previous categorisations of face muscles depending on sincerity or mendacity – is that it places the emphasis on why we use smiles.

The way in which smiles have been studied has employed a system of dividing the face up into different units of motor activity (called Action Units, or AUs), a system called the Facial Action Coding System, created by the psychologist Paul Ekman, who has undertaken some pioneering research in the field of emotional expression and deception and was the inspiration for the Cal Lightman character in the TV series, *Lie to Me* (Ekman used to write a blog after each episode explaining the "science" behind it, and it is worth seeking out; see, e.g., https://lietome.com/season-1/). Rychlowska et al. (2017) used this system to determine whether the three types of smiles were distinctive, finding that eyebrow flashes and zygomaticus major muscle contraction was associated with reward; lip pressing was indicative of affiliation; and asymmetrical zygomatic contraction and AUs associated with disgust (nose wrinkling, raising of upper lip) were characteristic of dominance. When people were then asked to look at animations of the different sorts of smiles and indicate what each signified, people could distinguish between dominance and reward smiles but were less adept at distinguishing between affiliation and reward smiles, which suggests that these two types of smiles are actually quite similar. In terms of the impression the smiles created, as you might expect, the affiliation and reward smiles were perceived as indicating more positivity and low dominance, whereas the dominance smile was perceived as less positive and less sociable. There is some research indicating that smiling during interviews is associated with better candidate evaluations and more positive hiring decisions in some job contexts but not others (Martin & Carlson, 2018 reviews this evidence); some research suggests that smiling is best deployed at the beginning and at the end of an interview – it should not be a permanent feature of the exchange, as that is likely to lead to some pretty strong, and negative, feedback from those judging candidates (Ruben, Hall & Schmid Mast, 2015).

There are some cultural differences in how these smiles are perceived. Rychlowska et al. (2015) asked respondents from nine countries to indicate the extent to which different types of intention lead to the production of specific smiles and produced similar results to those described earlier – people distinguished between smiles that reinforced, created social bonds or managed status. However, there were some nation-level differences, i.e., between those described as historically diverse (e.g., the United States and New Zealand) and those described as ethnically stable (e.g., Japan, Indonesia), where the former have seen considerable immigration, whereas the latter see much less. The former were more likely to indicate that smiles are used for affiliation; homogeneous nations are more likely to endorse the use of smiles to manage status (dominance). Men and adolescent boys tend to smile less than women and adolescent girls, but this difference depends on the context and the roles that each play (LaFrance, Hecht & Paluck, 2003). Men do sometimes smile more than do women under certain circumstances – when experiencing disgust, for example. Interestingly, La France et al. found a whole host of moderators for the general effect, including author sex. If the paper was first-authored by a man, men were reported to smile less than they were in papers first-authored by women, a finding the authors concede is inexplicable. Culture, nationality and age also moderated the findings – US and Canadian samples, for example, showed greater sex differences than did UK samples.

THE FACIAL FEEDBACK HYPOTHESIS

Before considering the role of smiling in the context of comedy, it is worth noting one particular phenomenon that was considered fairly stable and robust in psychology but has since turned out to be anything but. This is the facial feedback hypothesis. This suggests that our feelings and emotions are influenced by our facial expressions. There have been variations of this idea kicking around psychology since the days of James and Lange in the 19th and early 20th centuries, but perhaps the most famous demonstration was that of Strack, Martin and Stepper (1988) who asked people to rate the funniness and enjoyment of cartoons while they held a pencil either laterally between their teeth and lips or straight ahead as if they were sucking a straw, so the lips were pursed. A moment's reflection on this will tell you why – the former places your face's muscles in the position of a smile, whereas the latter places the lips pretty much in the position they would be if we sucked on a Fangtastic. Strack et al. found that people rated the cartoons as funnier and more enjoyable when the pen was held laterally between the teeth (and for the reason explained). This effect has been presented in countless textbooks, including mine. However, 17 labs have been unable to replicate this finding (Wagenmakers et al., 2016). So where does this leave the facial feedback hypothesis given that its posterchild appears to be made of quite flimsy material and appears to be coming off the wall? A recent meta-analysis by Coles, Larsen and Lench (2019) which examined 138 studies concluded that the pessimism may be unwarranted because while researchers tend to agree that the facial feedback hypothesis can be supported, the conditions under which it is supported have been the cause of controversy. The study did find a significant, but small, effect of facial feedback but also found that three aspects moderated this effect – facial feedback influenced emotional experience (how amused people were) and people's judgements of what they were looking at or listening to (how funny they found a cartoon, for example); facial feedback effects were larger if very emotionally arousing stimuli were absent; and facial feedback effects were larger with some types of stimuli (sentences vs. pictures).

LAUGHTER: WHAT IS IT?

The other major behavioural manifestation of enjoyment of humour and comedy is laughter. Or is it? The curious aspect of the literature on laughter is that research shows that most laughter is not evoked by jokes, or funny sayings or pratfalls or anything directly comical, but by everyday conversation (Provine, 2004). In meetings, one study found that 8.6% of vocalisations is spent laughing (Laskowski & Burger, 2007). Here are a few findings about laughter from the literature before we look in detail at the characteristics of laughter and the different types of laughter (and there are different types of laughter).

Provine (2004) reported that we are 30 times more likely to laugh with others than we are alone, suggesting that laughter is more social than anything else. Some evolutionary approaches to laughter have explained this by proposing that laughter was used as a way to signal tolerance and/or acceptance of non-serious play in others; this, in turn, could facilitate social interaction by widening the group and opening it up to playful exchanges. Curry and Dunbar (2013), in a less practical context, suggested that they found support for this in their study in which individuals who were found to show a mutual appreciation of the first lines of novels and jokes (which were in text form with the respondent's reaction to them written down) were more likely to find each other attractive. We also laugh more when we can see or hear someone laugh (Vlahovic, Roberts & Dunbar, 2012). According to Vettin and Todt (2004), we generate around five laughs for every 10 minutes of conversation, and this is a rate that we under-estimate (we think we generate fewer laughs). The person who laughs most in the conversation is the person who spoke last (Vettin & Todt, 2004), which suggests that laughter is not just a reaction to others but is something which is generated spontaneously and agentically. The box overleaf describes some of the findings from a study of the use of laughter in 29 six-person discussion groups, collected in the early 1980s from an American university.

One of the best, if not the most comprehensive, descriptions of laughter comes from a paper published in 1897. Here is how Hall and Allin summarised laughter:

> In the height of the laugh in some cases the chin quivers; the diaphragm movements are sometimes almost convulsive; some plant the elbows on the knees; others rock violently sideways, or more often back and forth; the hands are thrown into the air or clapped on the thighs; the face is distorted by various puckers, squints, wrinkles all over the forehead; lacks in symmetry, especially if there is embarrassment; the limbs jerk; the

foot is stamped; the fists pound; the face is sometimes distorted almost beyond recognition; waves of nervous tremor pass over the body; the face, neck and ears are red; the veins distended; the hand is placed over the eyes, mouth, or both; cheeks puff; some show every tooth, and one can see almost down the throat; the saliva flows; little children jump up and down, lying on the floor and roll all over the room; some swing the hands in the air; the breast heaves up and down; some turn around on the heel from left to right, or vice versa; the head shakes from side to side; many find it almost impossible to stop; about a dozen in our returns laugh with marked asymmetry; some show excessive surface of gums; others always hold the sides with both hands; others roll the head; features often twitch or tremble convulsively.

One of the most common acoustic manifestation of laughter are the noises represented by ho, he and ha. Laughter is an exhaltative action – it occurs when we exhale and the first syllable of noise produced is a fricative ("h") followed by a vowel (e.g., "a"), usually a central vowel where the tongue was placed halfway between a front vowel and a back vowel. In a study of the laughter of 97 young adults who watched funny films, the pitch of laughter was as high as 1245 Hz for men and 2083 Hz for women (Bachorowski, Smoski & Owren, 2001). Mittal and Yegnanarayana's (2015) very good review of the acoustics and linguistics of laughter noted that laughter can be analysed at various levels: episode, bout, call or segment. The first (episode) comprises two or more bouts of laughter separated by inspirations. A bout is audible laughter that occurs during an exhalation. A period of laughter contains a laugh cycle or pulses with pauses throughout (calls, shorter than bouts and which some have likened to the individual syllables of laughter; Owren, 2007). A bout has three components: onset, vocalisation and offset (the post-laughter part where a person's smile fades).

Laughter and humour in conversations

A study published in *Social Forces* in 2001 examined the use of humour in everyday conversation by measuring the duration of people's conversation –between the beginning of the conversation and a humorous event occurring – and the "spell duration" – the number of words between each "humorous event" (Robinson & Smith-Lovin, 2001). It also counted failed humour attempts, successful ones and non-humorous comments. From their sample of 29 discussions, they found 5640 speaker turns, and 375 of these were attempts at humour; half of these were successful attempts, according to the laughter produced. There were 13 attempts at humour per conversation, and individuals made, on average, about 2 attempts.

The average conversation was 2000 words long, and the study found that, after an initial spurt of jokes at the beginning, there was a gradual increase in humour attempts as the conversation progressed. When the researchers broke down the conversations into the beginning (first 400 words), middle (400 to1400 words) and end (>1400 words), the beginning and end sections included significantly more attempts at humour. Humour attempts that were successful and made people laugh were more likely to be followed by further humorous remarks, usually in the next turn after someone has made an attempt at humour. There was a sex difference, in the predictable direction. Men made more attempts, and more successful attempts, at humour than did women. The study also found that those who participated more were not more likely to make humour attempts than those who contributed less. However, they were more likely to engage in more successful humour attempts.

The researchers suggest that humour production is viewed as a positive and "powerful" behaviour and that those who make others laugh are more likely to be evaluated positively and as "powerful". This, they predict, means that high-status individuals will use more humour and make more successful attempts at humour than would low-status individuals (the boss vs. the employee, for example) and that a group member who has made people laugh will be permitted more opportunities to make people laugh. They view laughter and humour as having different effects depending on their role in the group. When humour is used explicitly in the context of the group (people make jokes about themselves, their organisation, their team, etc.), the researchers described this as "cohesion building" (humour as social glue). It builds as the conversation progresses and the group's identity becomes more unified. Group-feeling can be strengthened by joking about people outside the group (another team, organisation, ethnic group and so on). By contrast, "differentiating humour" describes that employed by a member of the group directed at members of the same group or even the person joking or making the funny remarks (inward or other-directed humour). Each type, the researchers predict, would be observed in different groups – the former in groups with low-status individuals; the latter in groups with high-status individuals. Men are more likely to be differentiators – the study found that 35% of men's humour was of this kind and 26% of women's. Women produced slightly more cohesive humour (56% of their attempts) than did men (50%), but the difference was small and not significant.

A distinction has been made between laughter that is produced in response to events (driven laughter) and laughter that is voluntary and has no clear elicitor (deliberate laughter). McGhee (1979) found that laughing was one of our first vocalisations after crying and is heard at around four months. After four months, the instances of laughter increase, especially between the second and third trimester (Sroufe & Wunsch, 1972). Tactile and auditory stimuli become less important elicitors of laughter as the children became older, whereas visual stimuli generated more laughter and consistently. Laughter is also heard in non-human primates such as chimpanzees, bonobos, orangutans and gorillas, although the contexts in which laughter is expressed differ from those of humans.

Ruch, Platt, Proyer and Chen (2019) have identified a number of factors that can generate types of laughter. These types are influenced by the "eliciting stimulus" (e.g., tickling), the "social situation" (the person you are with: friend, boss, etc.), "habitual/dispositional" (e.g., traits), "current affective states" (e.g., sexual interest), "organismic states" (being tired, drunk), and cognitive factors (presenting yourself, being aware of display rules).

Driven and deliberate/voluntary has not been the only taxonomy: there have been several. Bachorowski et al. (2001) identified three types of laugher bout: a song-like laugh (e.g., a giggle), a snorting unvoiced call (based around exhaling through the nose) and an unvoiced grunt laugh (pants and cackles). Owren and Bachorowski (2003) classed laughter into a voiced type (song-like bouts of laughter and giggles) and an unvoiced type characterised by open-mouthed breathy sounds, grunting with a closed mouth and snorting through the nose. Other taxonomies acknowledge laughter's role in speech and categorise conversational laughter as speech, speech-laughter and laughter (Menezes & Igarashi, 2006). Similarly, Kohler (2008) identified two types that occurred in conversation: in addition to speech-smile, there was speech-laugh and laughter. Tanaka and Campbell (2011) divided laughter into four phonetic types: voiced, chuckle, breathy ingression and nasal-grunt, and a later study (2014) divided laughter according to motivation – mirthful, polite, derisive and others – based on an analysis of Japanese speech patterns. Szameitat et al. (2009) also found that people could distinguish between laughter described as joy, tickling, taunting and schadenfreude. Laughter during tickling was rapid and high-pitched (1112 Hz in women; 528 Hz in men). Joyful laughter included more spaces between bouts. Schadenfreude was not associated with any specific, distinctive features. Taunting laughter had the lowest frequency. Comedy research is never straighforward.

LAUGHTER AS CONTAGION

In 1996, we published a paper on the effect of laughter in order to answer a question to which the literature had provided, at best, mixed answers (Martin & Gray, 1996). We know that laughter is contagious – given the right context, a persistent laugh or giggle will make us laugh. The interesting question is: Does the laughter make a joke or a person funnier, and do men and women respond differently? This question was raised by the British television producer, Paul Jackson (the production force behind *The Young Ones, Friday Night Live, Bottom, The Two Ronnies, Red Dwarf* and a slew of other popular comedies), when his sit-com *Happy Families* had not been successful. It was the work of Ben Elton, the prolific, motormouthed, co-writer of *The Young Ones* and effulgent compere of *Friday Night Live*, and his first solo outing as a sit-com writer. Jennifer Sanders played five different members of a family. Jackson noted that people had complained of a lack of jokes in the series, but, he argued, the show was stuffed with jokes but the problem was that "there was no laughter track to signal them in." In short, people would have found the series funnier had there been laughter present to signpost the jokes. But would they?

A small number of studies had tried to determine whether adding laughter (natural or canned) to a joke or a comedy routine could (1) increase the funniness and enjoyment of that joke/routine and (2) increase smiling and laughter. Natural laughter is an audience's voluntary laughter reaction to a comic stimulus; "canned" laughter is general, pre-recorded laughter which a producer will insert at relevant points of a comedy to signal that something funny is being said or done. It is canned because it is "in the can" (i.e., pre-recorded and in film cans). Canned laughter has few friends: in 1999, *Time* magazine declared this to be the worst idea of all time. It's been likened to muzak or aerosol cheese.

The effects of audience laugher are pretty consistent. Individuals listening to or watching a piece of comedy in the presence of audience laughter will rate the material as funnier than will those listening or watching without laughter present. They will also laugh more. Children who watched a slapstick film (Leventhal & Mace, 1970), college students who evaluated a cartoon (Cupchik & Leventhal, 1974) and participants who rated jokes (Chapman, 1973) laughed more when the stimuli were accompanied by laughter.

Some studies suggested that men and women (and boys and girls) respond differently to laughter: women find comedy funnier than do men when audience laughter is present (Cupchik & Leventhal, 1974;

Fuller & Sheehy-Skeffington, 1974; Leventhal & Cupchik, 1975; Smyth & Fuller, 1972). Both sexes respond similarly when no laughter is present. Other studies showed no sex differences (Butcher & Whissell, 1984; Chapman, 1973; Nosanchuk & Lightstone, 1976).

One reason for this inconsistency may have been the studies' ecological validity: Often, stimulus materials and the context in which they were presented were not particularly realistic. Presenting written jokes with canned laughter to participants or having an experimenter tell jokes, for example, are not realistic contexts. Different studies also administered different stimuli: such as pre-taped jokes, static cartoons, pre-taped anecdotes and blooper tapes.

As part of my undergraduate project at the University of Aberdeen, I set up an experiment to examine the effects of adding laughter to comedy in a context that was natural (Martin & Gray, 1996). Male and female undergraduates listened to a series of sketches from BBC Radio 4's *Arnold Brown and Company*, a topical comedy featuring live audience laughter. Half the group listened individually with laughter present on the audiotape and the other half listened individually to the same material with the laughter removed. The clips chosen were those which elicited the greatest laughter during the live show (so confirming that the material selected was perceived as funny). We measured participants' facial expression via an occluded video camera, their laughter via audio recording and their judgement of the comedy by asking them to complete measures of funniness and enjoyment. Participants in the laughter condition found the sketches funnier and more enjoyable than did those in the laughter absent condition. They also laughed significantly more. We found no differences between men and women – both sexes found the comedy funnier when there was laughter presented, and each produced comparable amounts of laughter and smiling.

The study generally supported the hypothesis that the presence of natural laughter can increase participant laughter and funniness judgements of comedy, and did so in a small group of young men and women using an audio recording. One explanation I put forward for this was the "attentional marker hypothesis". It predicts that when laughter is present, it draws attention to the material that is being listened to or watched. That is, it "marks out" a piece of comedy as being funny provided that the material is genuinely funny and tolerable. If the laughter draws attention to comedy that is not funny, then you might expect this comedy to result in less laughter and in being regarded as less funny because the laughter has drawn your attention to this very bad comedy.

The laughter as contagion phenomenon has particular traction in groups and couples. Studies have shown that laughter expressed vocally or portrayed in photographs is associated with increased likeability of the person doing the laughing (Reysen, 2006). Laughter during an interaction leads to much greater satisfaction with that interaction (Vlahovic et al., 2012). Dezecache and Dunbar (2012) in a naturalistic study of people in bars found that the presence of laughter produced a threefold increase in the likelihood of bonding. People are also very adept at distinguishing between involuntary and voluntary laughs. Bryant and Aktipis (2014) found that people could distinguish between spontaneous and volitional laughter, and when laugh speed was increased, both types of laughter were perceived as being more natural.

BEING VIEWED

Anyone exposed to, or who grew up with, American sitcoms will be familiar with the pre-credits refrain that such and such a show "is filmed in front of a live studio audience". It sends a message that the laughter isn't canned but genuine and sincere and not artificially added. In a TV recording like this, the cameras are pointing one way – at the actors, not the audience. But what if the cameras are pointed at the audience as well? Would this influence the degree of laughter it produced or affect how funny its members thought the comedy was?

Many programmes do include this device – an audience reaction of laughter acts as visual confirmation that the host's or programme's content is funny. It is also important in the context of research – comedy research which measures laughter or smiling will employ some recording device. Until the early 1990s, no study had seriously considered whether the presence of these devices would inhibit (or facilitate) or leave unaffected people's behavioural responses and their judgements about comedy's funniness. We wanted to investigate whether the medium of comedy (written, audio, audio-visual) and being overtly or covertly video-taped influenced participants' responses to comedy (Martin, Sadler, Barrett & Beven, 2008). The material we used was the "Dish and Dishonesty" episode from the BBC2 sitcom *Blackadder III* starring Rowan Atkinson as the cynical, oppressed but manipulative lackey of George III (this was the conceit of all the Blackadder series – Edmund Blackadder was a Machiavellian second-fiddle supporting role in each series, besieged and frustrated by stupidity and misfortune in whichever epoch he found himself in). This episode was a clever satire on the rotten boroughs which existed in England at a time when corruption was rife and election to Parliament was greased more by money and connections than ability and probity. The series lent itself well to study because it was available in three media: as published scripts, as audiocassette and as video. We used an approximately 15-minute segment of the series (and the equivalent portion of text for the text-only condition) and recorded participants' facial expressions either overtly with the camera within sight or covertly where the camera was placed behind a two-way mirror. All participants were aware they were being video-recorded.

Audio and audio-visual comedy was associated with more smiling and laughter than was the text (predictably and predicted); there was no difference between the audio and audio-visual media. Media had no significant effect on how enjoyable or funny people found the comedy. The presence of a camera did have an effect – when the camera was present, participants laughed less and found the comedy less enjoyable. The study found two important results: that the medium of comedy you use may not necessarily affect the cognitive judgements of your participants (they may find the media equally funny/enjoyable) but will affect expressive responses such as laughter and smiling. It also found that the presence of a camera can inhibit some responses, and this is worth considering when conducting humour experiments involving the video recording of participants.

TICKLING

Of course, the only guaranteed way of provoking laughter is to tickle someone but the person has to either want to be tickled or be grudgingly willing to be tickled – it would be odd for a loathsome boss or an unwelcome lounge lizard or the person delivering your post to start palpating your waist, soles or knees. You likely would not be cheery. It is also true that it is very difficult to tickle yourself (although not impossible), probably because as Provine (2004) has noted, if it wasn't, we would be accidentally tickling ourselves all day. By the same token, however, we can't really tell ourselves a joke and make ourselves laugh either, unless we're creating the joke for the first time and the novelty makes us laugh.

The affective and motor response that results from someone else tickling you is greater, much greater, than if you attempted the same ticking on yourself. The anticipation of tickling can also lead to a similar affective response to that generated when you're physically tickled. Similar brain regions might also be involved. Carlsson, Petrovic, Skare, Petersson and Ingvar (2000), for example, used functional magnetic resonance imaging (fMRI) to measure brain activation during actual tickling and the anticipation of being tickled and found that both recruited similar areas, including increased activation in the primary sensory cortex on the opposite side that was tickled (anticipated to be tickled), both sides of the inferior parietal lobe, the secondary somatosensory cortex, the right anterior cingulate cortex and part of the right prefrontal cortex and decreases in the sensory and motor cortices unrelated to tickling. The authors, correctly, caution that their participants were asked to inhibit themselves because they were inside a brain scanner and these are sensitive to motor movement, meaning that they cannot detect a good signal if the head is moving. Some of the activation may, therefore, be attributable to this inhibition rather than tickling itself. An fMRI study published almost

20 years later, investigated the anticipated tickling of the foot in 31 healthy adults (Wattendorf et al., 2019). When people anticipated tickling, different areas from those reported in the earlier study were activated, including the anterior insula, hypothalamus, the nucleus accumbens and ventral tegmental area, with decreases in the globus pallidus. The activation in the insula predicted the amount of laughter during actual tickling: the greater the activation during anticipation, the greater the laughter. Actual tickling activated similar areas and the anterior cingulate cortex, posterior insula and periaqueductal grey area.

Sometimes, not knowing where the tickling will occur just adds to the anticipation, something which Darwin noted when he said that "from the fact that a child can hardly tickle itself, or in a much less degree than when tickled by another person, it seems that the precise point to be touched must not be known", although we don't need to know where or when we'll be tickled in order to respond to it. The American Journal of Psychology in 1897 reported, as we saw earlier, one of the first studies of tickling and laughter with, for the time, a huge sample (N = 700) and made many of the observations described here. More recent studies have found the tickling is more likely to be done by a member of the opposite sex (see Provine, 2004). It is much less common after the age of 40 presumably because our retinues of ticklers have receded. One study found that people who regarded themselves as ticklish were more likely to say they smiled, laughed and giggled more (Fridlund & Loftis, 1990). Tickling leads to laughter, and this is thought to represent a release of tension built up by the tickling, and this (tension release) represents one view of why tickling leads to laughter. This notion is reviewed in the next chapter.

MEASURING A SENSE OF HUMOUR

Psychologists measure. They measure brain activation, personality, intelligence, body mass index, your attitudes – all sorts of things. They have also found ways of measuring the sense of humour. But what is a "sense of humour"? It is a question that is in terms of difficulty in answering probably only second to "What is love?" or "Where did I leave my pen?"

Various thinkers have attempted to distil the essence of a sense of humour, but a universally accepted definition has escaped science. Eysenck (1942) proposed that we use the phrase to describe (1) a person who makes others laugh, (2) a person who laughs a lot or is easily amused or (3) a person who tells funny jokes to amuse others. Hehl and Ruch (1985) expanded on this last conception and cited seven behaviours or traits which might constitute a sense of humour, including the understanding of jokes, how humour is expressed, the appreciation of humour and the use of humour as a coping mechanism. Martin (2003) succinctly summed it up in the following way: "a personality trait or individual difference variable (or more likely a family of related traits or variables)", which includes the ability to appreciate, create and comprehend humour.

A widely used – although not the only – measure of the sense of humour has been Martin, Puhlik-Doris, Gray and Weir's (2013) Humor Styles Questionnaire (HSQ). This is a 32-item questionnaire which measures four styles of humour, validated on 300 undergraduates at, one presumes given the authors' affiliations, a Canadian university. The four styles are "Self-enhancing" (described as "relatively benign uses of humour to enhance the self"), "Affiliative" (the use of humour to enhance relationships with others), "Aggressive" ("the use of humour to enhance relationships at the expense of others) and "Self-defeating" ("the use of humour to enhance relationships at the expense of the self"). Some examples of the types of statements included in the questionnaire to measure each style are found in Table 1.2.

People who score high on Affiliative humour enjoy saying funny things and telling jokes, doing this to enhance their relationships or to reduce animosity; they do not take themselves too seriously. Self-enhancing humour is characterised by having a generally humorous disposition and view of life, "a tendency to be frequently amused by the incongruities of life, and to maintain a humorous perspective even in the face of stress or adversity" (p. 53), thus making it the

Table 1.2 Examples of statements measuring each humour style on the HSQ (Martin et al., 2013)

Affiliative humour	I laugh and joke a lot with my closest friends
	I rarely make other people laugh by telling funny stories about myself (this item is reversed in the calculation of the score)
	I enjoy making people laugh
Self-enhancing humour	If I am feeling depressed, I can usually cheer myself up with humor
	Even when I am by myself, I am often amused by the absurdities of life
	If I am feeling upset or unhappy I usually try to think of something funny about the situation to make myself feel better
Aggressive humour	If someone makes a mistake, I will often tease them about it
	People are never offended or hurt by my sense of humor (reversed item)
	When telling jokes or saying funny things, I am usually not very concerned about how other people are taking it
Self-defeating humour	I let people laugh at me or make fun at my expense more than I should
	I will often get carried away in putting myself down if it makes my family or friends laugh
	I often try to make people like or accept me more by saying something funny about my own weaknesses, blunders, or faults

closest of the types to involve using humour as a coping mechanism. Aggressive humour involves the negative application or production of humour in the form of cutting wit, sarcasm, ridicule or disparagement and with little or no regard for the consequence of such application or production. Often, it is deliberate but it can also describe a person who is unable to prevent themselves from saying what they believe to be funny regardless of what the impact may be on the recipient.

Finally, Self-defeating humour describes a style of humour characterised by the use of humour as a self-effacement device to ingratiate oneself with others, to receive the approval of others and demonstrate a willingness to be the victim of others' jokes about them. Martin et al. also characterise this style as being deflective in that the person utilising this type of humour will use it to mask or to avoid their concern or resistance to a particular point of view, issue or person, or to avoid the discussion of difficult issues. In Martin et al.'s measure development study of 470 men and 725 women, men and women were similar (although statistically different) in terms of affiliative, self-defeating and self-enhancing humour, but men scored much higher (seven points higher) than did women for aggressive humour, a common finding in the literature. The scale also correlated positively and highly with four other measures commonly used in this type of research – the SHRQ, CHS, SHQ-6 and MSHS (described later) – but most of this relationship was attributable to two dimensions: Affiliative humour and Self-enhancing humour.

OTHER WAYS OF "MEASURING" HUMOUR

The appendix of Wilibald Ruch's comprehensive book, *The Sense of Humour*, lists over 50 different measures of humour and includes categories such as "jokes and cartoon tests", "self-report scales" (such as those described next), "children humor tests" and examples of more esoteric types (the Marital Interaction Coding System includes a humour scale). One widely used questionnaire is the Situational Humor Response Questionnaire (SHRQ; Martin & Lefcourt, 1984), which measures how likely we are to smile and laugh in 18 different social scenarios; another is the Coping Humor Scale (CHS; Martin & Lefcourt, 1983), which measures the degree we are likely to use humour to cope with life's difficulties and stresses. The Sense of Humor Questionnaire (SHQ-6; Svebak, 1996) is a brief measure which asks people how they encounter humour in their lives and how they produce it, whereas the Multidimensional Sense of Humor Scale (MSHS; Thorson & Powell, 1993) is a similar measure to the HSQ and also produces a four-factor structure (that is, there are four bunches of statements, and within each bunch the items correlate with each other, suggesting that they measure a common theme or factor).

And this is just the tip of the iceberg, but a very visible tip because these are the scales you will see most widely used and reported. A recent addition to this panoply is the comic styles and comic style markers developed by Ruch and his colleagues (Heintz & Ruch, 2019; Ruch, Heintz, Platt, Wagner & Proyer, 2018). Based largely on material from literature (fiction), these styles comprise fun, (benevolent) humour, nonsense, wit, irony, satire, sarcasm and cynicism. The idea behind the formulation is that we use a specific humour style more often than others, and this helps identify individual differences in humour use. There are also relationships between these and the HSQ. Correlations are found between the fun style and affiliative humour, between the benevolent style and self-enhancing and between the sarcasm style and aggressive humour. You'll see that four of these styles are what you might think of as reflecting dark traits and four reflect lighter traits (fun and nonsense, for example). They are yet another way of characterising how we use humour, but whether they are any more useful or informative than existing measures remains to be seen.

CONCLUSION

This chapter has reviewed some of the basic machinery of comedy and humour – what these are and how they might be produced and how they affect us. Before we look at the individual characteristics that might influence our response to comedy, the next chapter examines the theories that various philosophers and scientists have proposed to explain humour, comedy and laughter.

2

THEORIES OF COMEDY AND LAUGHTER

"What," asked Henri Bergson in *Laughter: An Essay on the Meaning of the Comic* (1911), "does laughter mean? What is the basal element in the laughable? What common good can we find between the grimace of the merry-andrew, a play upon words, an equivocal situation, a burlesque, or a scene of high comedy? A pert challenge flung at philosophic speculation". If you can say one thing about philosophical speculators, they love pert challenges. And speaking of pert, a "merry-andrew" is a person who entertains others comically.

Few things divide and bring together comedy researchers more than theories of comedy, and there is plenty to help with the division. According to one source, even up until the early 1920s, some 77 variants of theories of humour existed (Greig, 1923). As Moreall (1986) noted, so many situations can provoke laughter that they have nothing in common apart from laughter – some examples include responding to comedy, winning a game, being tickled, seeing a magic trick, experiencing embarrassment, solving a puzzle, regaining safety, and others.

With this in mind, theories of humour/comedy/laughter have roughly fallen into three camps: theories of superiority, theories of incongruity and theories of arousal and energy release. There is another theory, reversal theory, that has also attracted some

DOI: 10.4324/9780429347269-2

attention. Whether these are theories in the strictest sense though is arguable – a good theory, as Martin (2006) reaffirms, needs to be clearly defined, cites necessary and sufficient conditions and should be falsifiable. It is fair to say that none of the theories described here meet these criteria fully.

THEORY OF SUPERIORITY (DISPARAGEMENT HUMOUR)

The first theory of humour and laughter was proposed by Plato, and it was the first example in what has become known as superiority theory: the use of humour to belittle others and the creation of amusement by having the inferiority of others made salient to us. This is the pthonic (or malicious) element of humour. Humour and laughter are a form of aggression – instrumental aggression – in that the humour and laughter serve a deliberate and conscious purpose. According to Plato's *Philebus*, we laugh at vice and the ignorance of people. It reflects a malicious way of thinking about others, and we derive our amusement from this. In the *Republic*, he proposed that references to the gods and heroes overcome by laughter should be expunged, an idea which led to the central theme of Umberto Eco's novel *The Name of the Rose*, in which laughter was considered verboten.

Socrates, Plato's senior, held a similar view, arguing that malicious men are pleased with their neighbour's misfortunes. "The ridiculous", wrote Socrates, "is a certain kind of evil", presciently predicting Adam Sandler films 2000 years before they happened. The weak who are unable to retaliate when they are laughed at are ridiculous. In his *Dialogue with Protarchus*, Socrates wrote that laughing at one's friends brings pleasure but also pain because we are mixing malice with laughter.

To complete the triad of ancient scholars' views on mirth, Aristotle held similar views to his tutors and held some pointedly ripe views (at least in translation) of people who used humour, describing them as "vulgar buffoons". He also argued that amusement arose from regarding others as inferior (Aristotle also observed that laughter could be a response to different types of ambiguity, and we'll return to this later). "Comedy", he wrote in *Poetics*, "is an imitation of people who are worse than average. The ridiculous [the people] is a species of ugly; it may be defined as a mistake or unseemliness". Aristotle did acknowledge some subtleties of difference: those who couldn't think of anything funny to say are perceived as dour and boorish; those who joke in a tactful way are called witty, implying a "quick versatility", so Aristotle was an equal opportunities judge. Warming to his theme, Aristotle continues, "the buffoon cannot resist any temptation to be funny . . . he says no things no cultivated man would say . . . the boor is useless in social relations . . . he contributes nothing and takes offence at everything". We'll return to buffoons in the chapter on comedians.

Superiority theory, and we'll examine variants of it shortly, supports the controversial notion that all humour, in some way, has a victim and that any joke, if you interpret it strictly enough, has a victim and an agent that overcomes and overpowers (even if the "victim" or the "agent" are inanimate). This is the view of Gruner, who has argued that jokes contain winners and losers, even self-deprecating ones, perhaps especially self-deprecating ones. He and others have noted the degree of aggression in jokes that involve sex and race or scatology, and these are the types of jokes that are divisive and have very clear victims who the jokes expects us to laugh at – whether it is the hen-pecked husband, the dumb blonde or the dim Irishman (and it is usually a man). Of course, the victim may merit the "victimhood": jokes or humour which are designed to engender a sense of belonging or community in the face of unfathomable evil, for example. By laughing at an aggressor, the aggression, pain or malice conducted by the aggressor is reduced or mollified. It is a way of coping, in Kaller's (1968; cited in Ruch, 2010) words: "I laugh at that which has endangered or degraded or has fought to suppress and enslave and destroy what I cherish." This is an example of the use of disparagement to achieve an ostensibly noble end, although it does also illustrate a competing theory of laughter, which is that humour provides a form of cathartic or psychic release. This type of humour may help us cope better with adversity, and there is a particular type of humour that exemplifies this: gallows humour, a term coined by

Freud. Here, humour is used as "emotional anaesthesia" (McDougall, 1903), a means of numbing painful thoughts.

The most well-developed superiority theory of humour was developed by Thomas Hobbes (1588–1679) who described laughter as an expression of "sudden glory". At the core of this theory was the very worst interpretation of human nature – that we revel in the failures of others and we seek people who are less than we are to make fun of. We do this because life is a struggle for success and domination and power. It is a bleak and cactopian view but one that is reflected in the use of much humour. "Men laugh at the infirmities of others", Hobbes wrote, "the passion of laughter is nothing else but sudden glory arising from some sudden conception of some eminency in ourselves, by comparison with the infirmity of others, or with our own formerly"; the latter phrase suggests that we can laugh at our (previously inferior) selves. Descartes (1596–1650), who had little specific to say on humour and laughter, but did propose a physiological explanation of laughter (expulsion of air from the lungs caused by the flow of blood from the lungs to the heart), tilted towards superiority theory when he addressed the nature of scorn in *The Passions of the Soul*. Scorn or derision, he argued, "is a sort of joy mingled with hatred, which proceeds from our perceiving some small evil in a person whom we consider deserving it; we have joy in seeing it is him who is deserving of it". Descartes listed some of the objects of abuse and scorn: the "lame, blind of eye, hunch-backed or have received some public insult", illustrating, as if illustration were needed, that the abuse directed at those who look different, particularly those who exhibit some deformity, is nothing new.

A critic of Hobbes, Frances Hutcheson (1694–1740), argued that there was little connection between superiority and being amused and that being comic is the ability to create inappropriate metaphors and similes. This represents the beginning of the idea of incongruity, a theory discussed next. Hutcheson argued that there are "innumerable instances of laughter where no person is ridiculed nor does he who laughs compare himself to anything". Instead, "the cause of laughter is the bringing together of images which have contrary additional ideas". The contrast between ideas of grandeur and ideas of meanness creates amusement: "the greatest part of our raillery and jest is founded upon it".

Superiority theory is thought to explain why some people use disparaging humour – and some of the research in this area is reviewed in the next chapters, especially research that has focused on ethnicity and sex (and sexism). The relationship is complicated in that some studies report that men and women enjoy comedy that disparages women more than comedy that disparages men. La Fave, Haddad and Maesen's (1976) vicarious superiority theory and Zillmann and Cantor's (1976) dispositional theory both share the view that the amusement we experience when responding to disparagement humour is conditional on the attitude we hold towards the subject of the disparagement, i.e., our degree of prejudice. We are more likely to be amused when the subject – or more pertinently, the object – is the "out-group". A study of US presidential primary and election debates found that humour was principally directed at out-groups and the opposition (Stewart, 2012; Stewart et al., 2018). The identification of a defect, however, is not sufficient; we must experience a sense of relief that we do not express or exhibit this defect.

Disparagement humour is designed to undermine and, by undermining, it may initiate, consolidate or exacerbate prejudice or might lead to the development of negative stereotypes. And lots of these stereotypes are used in disparaging humour, involving sex, culture, ethnicity, professions and phyla. Although disparagement humour is aggressive, it may not necessarily involve physical aggression, although it can. The hoary joke "What do you call 100 lawyers at the bottom of the ocean? A start" is an exemplar of the genre. Others are directed at sex, hair colour or parts of the world: examples are many (e.g., "How do you get a one-handed blonde down from a tree? Wave at her"; "What's the difference between an Essex girl and a limousine? Not everybody has been in a limo"; "What do you call a sheep tied to a lamp post in Cardiff? A leisure centre" and so on).

Studies – few but some – have found that disparagement humour directed towards some groups (lawyers, for example) can lead listeners to report more negative attitudes towards lawyers. Canadians were also reported to hold more negative views of Newfoundlanders after reading disparaging, funny comments about this group (Maio, Olson & Bush, 1997). But other studies have found no negative effects of exposure to disparagement humour (Olson, Maio & Hobden, 1999).

INCONGRUITY THEORY

A strong theory of humour which also has a long history is incongruity theory. This argues that humour which is unpredictable and which involves the juxtaposition of opposing ideas, thoughts or actions will generate mirth. This misapprehension was well-observed by Voltaire, who remarked in *L'Enfant Prodigue*, that "in the theatre there is almost never a general outburst of laughter except on the occasion of a misapprehension". One of my most favourite illustrations of this is a Pilbrow cartoon in which two firefighters attend the scene of an incident involving a tree inserted into an irritated cat's anus. One firefighter says to the other: "Well, I suppose a tree stuck up a cat makes a change." Another favourite line is the opening of Martin Amis's first novel, *The Rachel Papers*: "My name is Charles Highway although you probably wouldn't think it to look at me." What does he look like? What does a Charles Highway look like? Is he nice? Fans of Robin Halstead, Jason Hazeley, Alex Morris and Joel Morris's *The Framley Examiner* will recognise that the periodical is wall-to-wall incongruity (a typical small ad: "LOST: Mind. Framley area, Thurs. Believed blown. Box FE 7611"). In the recurring "History Today" sketch by David Baddiel and Rob Newman from *Newman and Baddiel in Pieces*, the comedians play two dusty history academics in a TV studio discussion where the staid and sober set-up – about some arcane detail or event in history – always ends up with them bickering and arguing like children ("That's your mum, that is").

Cicero (106–143) was one of the first to identify incongruity as a source of humour. "The most common kind of joke", he wrote, "is that in which we expect one thing and another is said: here our own disappointed expectation makes us laugh. But if something ambiguous is thrown in, too, the effect of the joke is heightened", which, although written almost 2000 years ago, perfectly encapsulates incongruity. But perhaps the greatest "modern" proponent of incongruity was Arthur Schopenhauer (1788–1860). In *The World As Will and Idea*, he argued that humour arose from a clash between our sensory knowledge of things and our abstract knowledge of those things, specifically "the cause of laughter in every case is simply the sudden perception of the incongruity between a concept and the real object . . . the greater and more unexpected this incongruity is, the more violent will be the laughter".

And comedy is festooned with examples of this. Monty Python is a well-known example with its dead parrot, Spanish Inquisition, a Messiah who is not the Messiah and a Colonel who interrupts sketches because they are too silly. The TV series *Police Squad* and the film *Airplane!* trade on little else but incongruity (you might remember that Jim Abrahams, David Zucker and Jerry Zucker's short-lived TV precursor to their films, a spoof of American TV police procedurals, would open with the title of that night's episode, but the announcer would read a different episode title). Another example is one of Bob Monkhouse's most famous jokes: "I want to die like my father, peacefully in his sleep, not screaming and terrified, like his passengers". And here is an example from Jo Brand: "I was not a particularly small child. I was the one who always got picked to play Bethlehem in the school nativity". Clive James famously likened Arnold Schwarzenegger to a condom stuffed with walnuts.

A similar but stronger view of incongruity was published virtually contemporaneously by William Hazlitt (1178–1830). In lectures on the English comic writers (1885) he wrote: "the essence of the laughable then is the incongruous, the disconnecting one idea from another, or the jostling of one feeling against the other". He also noted that humans, unlike other species, laughed and wept and were the only animals "struck with the difference between what things are, and what they ought to be". He identified three degrees of the "laughable": the short-lived surprise at something happening, the ludicrousness of something improbable or distressing and ridiculousness arising out of sheer absurdity, and he also gave examples: children, deformity and people dressing fashionably whether the clothes were in fashion or not. In short, humour was "an imitation of the natural or acquired absurdities of mankind", according to Hazlitt.

Incongruity also formed the cornerstone of Soren Kierkegaard's (1813–1855) theory of laughter, identifying contradiction as being the core element of comedy and humour: "Wherever there is life, there is contradiction, and wherever there is contradiction, the comical is present". Recall Ayckbourn's quote at the beginning about comedy and tragedy, and Kierkegaard made a similar point. "The tragic and the comic are the same insofar as both are based on contradiction", he wrote, "but the tragic is suffering contradiction; the comical, the painless contradiction", thus making the other important point that contradiction itself does not automatically lead to mirth. Alexander Bain had listed some of the incongruities which would definitely not arouse mirth: a man under a heavy burden, an out-of-tune instrument, a fly in ointment, snow in May, a corpse at a feast . . . although if you examine any of these even cursorily, they can unravel pretty quickly. Les Dawson's discordant piano playing and Eric Morcambe's similar crime against the piano in front of Andre Previn are good examples of the second, and a variety of films and TV programmes have mined the potential of the corpse as a comedic device.

Koestler (1964) couched the relationship in more technical terms. He used the term "bisociation" to describe a situation, event or idea where a similarity is perceived between them but the perceiver is aware that two self-consistent truths are incompatible. A single event is "made to vibrate simultaneously on two different wavelengths", and the core of humour is the activation of two incompatible perceptions. Koestler's idea led to more specific models such as Shultz's (1977) incongruity-resolution theory in which punchlines, being incongruous, lead the reader, listener or viewer to go back over the joke to search and confirm the ambiguity (modern researchers have examined how and when the brain does this; see Chapter 7). Suls's (1972, 1983) two-stage model of humour comprehension also incorporates incongruity in that it proposes that as we hear a joke, we make predictions about the outcome of what we are being told based on the premise. If the prediction is wrong, we try and figure out why, and when we do figure this out, the incongruity disappears and we laugh. If we don't, then we don't get the joke and we don't laugh. Of course, if a joke were genuinely logical, then a joke would be a puzzle, not a joke, as others have pointed out. Incongruity resolution appears to be at the heart of most jokes. One study conducted a factor analysis of various jokes and discovered that the first factor that emerged was cognitive incongruity, followed by superiority, then some emotional element (pain or importance). The funniness ratings participants provided loaded on the first factor – it predicted how funny people thought the jokes were (Wicker, Thorelli, Barron III & Ponder, 1981). Whether you can have humour generated by incongruity without resolution is a moot point, and some have argued that you can. It is also worth noting that the most wildly incongruous jokes are not necessarily the funniest. Predictable, but still incongruous, endings are judged to be funnier.

RELIEF THEORY

Some theories view laughter as a way of releasing built-up energy. Perhaps the clearest example of this theory is Freud's. Freud viewed humour and laughter as an outlet for excessive psychic or nervous energy. In *Jokes and Their Relation to the Unconscious*, he argued that there were three situations in which laughter occurs: joking, the comic and humour, and cited all manner of fictional unconscious mechanisms to explain why these occur. He refers to the superego, ego and the id, naturally, but he may just as well have been referring to pixies. These structures, via jokes, allow the expression of thoughts and feelings that would otherwise be suppressed. Tendentious jokes – those involving hostility or sex – would be most likely to provoke this expression. Jokes require "joke work" (cognitive techniques) and the expression of repressed impulses. The distraction of the superego, which polices our thoughts and desires, leads to the expression of sexual or aggressive impulses derived from the id, the John Belushi of the unconscious. Throughout the 1960s and 1970s, there were several attempts to test some of the hypotheses that could be derived from the theory, but these met with mixed results.

AROUSAL THEORY

Freud's theory was inspired by another thinker, Herbert Spencer (1860), who argued that our system of emotional expression was similar to a hydraulic system in that energy is built up and is released through movement. In comedy and humour, that movement is laughter, and laughter permits the release of this built-up energy. The most widely discussed theory of arousal is that of Berlyne (1960, 1969, 1972). Although this theory was developed in the context of creativity and the appreciation of aesthetics, its principal thrust is that works of art express collective variables, the features which make the work desirable and pleasing. Some of these variables include novelty, complexity, surprise, ambiguity and incongruity, and we look for and appreciate combinations of these. These features are also clearly features of jokes. Unlike Freud, Berlyne did not view laughter as a release of tension. Instead, he proposed an inverted U-shaped process of arousal where moderate amounts of arousal would provoke the most pleasure, but too little or too much would be displeasing. He cited two mechanisms to explain this: the arousal boost and the arousal jag. The boost is present when, for example, we are listening to a joke and appreciating its collective variables. The arousal they create reaches a level that is optimal and pleasant. If the arousal persists, it becomes aversive. This is the jag. The punchline in a joke helps reduce the arousal and leaves the listener in a pleasurable state. Does the theory explain why we laugh and respond to humour?

Not fully. Studies that have tested the predictions from the model have found conflicting results. Some studies, for example, have found that negative and positive arousal can increase the funniness of humour (contrary to what the theory predicts). The boost element probably has more support than does the jag element – punchlines, for example, tend to increase arousal rather than decrease it (and these can be measured physiologically via skin conductance or heart rate).

REVERSAL THEORY

The final major theory of humour and laughter recognises how important play is in humour. That is, it is a playful activity (Apter, 1982;

Apter & Smith, 1977). Apter, as you saw in Chapter 1, argued that in order to appreciate humour, we have to be in a playful state of mind, we have to be receptive to the comedy. He called this state our "protective frame" or a "psychological safety zone", a "private" world where we can explore, unfettered by inhibition and judgement. Apter distinguished between this state – which he called the paratelic state – and the serious, unplayful, more goal-directed state – which he called the telic state. The latter is situated in the future, it is a state in which we have to reach goals undistracted. The former is situated in the present and not related to any goal; behaviour is enjoyed for what it is, not for what it can achieve. We switch between these states throughout the day, hence "reversal" theory. In the telic state, high arousal is aversive and causes anxiety; the paratelic state's low arousal causes boredom, and high arousal causes excitement. Unlike incongruity theory, this theory does not argue that incongruity resolution is not required in humour appreciation, only a recognition of the incongruity (Apter used the term "synergy" to describe two contradictory thoughts about the same object). The ridiculousness of the object that we see in this synergy or incongruity makes it feel less important and we regard it more playfully. The theory was developed to take into account social contexts by Wyer and Collins (1992). The comprehension elaboration theory of humour tries to explain how humour is used in social interactions: how it is understood and used. Wyer and Collins argued that humour is more enjoyable if we have to expend cognitive effort (the elaboration). A similar theory was proposed by Moreall, who argued that laughter is the result of pleasure created by the perception of psychological shifts: from negative/non-emotional states to positive emotional states, for example.

CONCLUSION

These are some of the major theories of laughter and humour that have been developed over the centuries, and there many more – and more specific theories – which are essentially variants of these theories. Does one explain all of humour, comedy and laughter? No. But of all the theories described here, the theory of incongruity does explain a lot of what makes us laugh.

3

INDIVIDUAL DIFFERENCES IN HUMOUR: SEX, PERSONALITY, INTELLIGENCE AND CULTURE

SEX, HUMOUR AND COMEDY

Here's a diverse set of headlines for you: "Why Women Aren't Funny" (*Vanity Fair*), "Women Just Aren't Funny" (*The New Yorker*), "Why Men Don't Like Funny Women" (*The Atlantic*), "Reasons Women Aren't Funny" (*McSweeneys*) and let us not forget the 2014 documentary, *Women Aren't Funny*. You might be beginning to detect some sort of pattern.

The notion that one sex might be funnier than another (or, more tendentiously, that one sex is less funny than another) is a familiar media trope designed to court some sporadic misandry or misogyny. The notion that women cannot be objectively funny is self-evidently falsifiable – from Lucille Ball, Roseanne Barr, *The Golden Girls*, Joan Rivers, Julia Louis-Dreyfus, Kathy Burke, Sarah Millican and Victoria Wood to Jo Brand, Rebel Wilson, Laura Solon, Tracey Ullman, French and Saunders, Miranda Hart, Amy Schumer and the raft of *Saturday Night Live* alumna (Kirsten Wiig, Gilda Radner, Kate McKinnon, Tina Fey), this tiny, selective list demonstrates that what is glib isn't always true. *Bridesmaids*, released in 2011 with an all-woman principal cast and written by Kirsten Wiig and Annie Mumolo, made $300 million and represented something of a breakthrough in terms of female-dominated

DOI: 10.4324/9780429347269-3

comedy films. Tina Fey (with Alec Baldwin) dominates 30 *Rock* as Julia Louis-Dreyfus dominates *Veep*.

Viv Goskrop, a journalist who spent a large part of a year training to be a stand-up comedian scrabbling and scratching for gigs and open mics (performing 100 gigs in 100 consecutive days), wrote about her experiences on the gruelling comedy circuit in her book, *I Laughed, I Cried*. She describes how exhilarating the experience was but also how "reckless, masochistic and destructive" it was, placing great pressure on her marriage ("I came to realise that you can push someone a long way and see that they don't break", she wrote, "but that doesn't mean that you should keep pushing them. More likely it teaches you that you were wrong to push them that far in the first place"). She recounts little sexism on the circuit, although she does describe some greasy encounters with some very touchy men after these gigs. A discussion of female comedians and comedy in *The What the Frock! Book of Funny Women*, on the other hand, raises some of the issues women encounter in comedy, as have some more recent media reports (www.theguardian.com/stage/2020/aug/05/creepy-uncom fortable-sexism-harassment-assault-faced-by-female-standups). Morwenna Banks and Amanda Swift's book *The Joke's on Us* provides a similar, thorough and thoughtful account of the role of women comedians – interviewing many – and how this role has developed since the 19th century. It's prefaced with a quote from an anonymous BBC Light Entertainment producer: "Women in comedy? That'll be a very short book". There are unfunny women and there are unfunny men, and that is one glib statement that is true.

We know – because the literature almost universally reports it – that men are more likely to produce humour than are women (Green-gross & Miller, 2011; Myers, Ropog & Rodgers, 1997; Robinson & Smith-Lovin, 2001). It is one of the more consistent findings in the psychology of comedy, akin to the finding in the psychology of horror that men are more likely than women to like and seek out horror content (Martin, 2019). Myers et al. found that men made more attempts at humour, regarded their attempts to be more effective than did women and used humour in a more negative way than did women.

There may also be disadvantages to women using humour: Evans, Slaughter, Ellis and Rivin (2019) found that when men expressed humour in a work-based context (participants watched a video of a fictional manager who was either a man or a woman), this was regarded as functional; when a women did the same, it was considered to be disruptive and her status was perceived as lower than that of her male equivalent. The authors interpret this finding in the context of parallel constraint satisfaction theory, which argues that when we form impressions in ambiguous circumstances, we use stereotype knowledge, and this and the observed behaviour constrain our perception of the person. As agency is a stereotypical male trait, they argue that men are more likely to be perceived as dominant and confident (and, therefore, use humour), and this information constrains their perception of a humorous man (and woman).

A more interesting discussion, however, revolves around whether sex differences exist in more specific bailiwicks of comedy and humour. That is, whether there is evidence that one sex is funnier than the other. Do men and women prefer different types of comedy, and do the sexes respond (behaviourally) differently to comedy, i.e., does one sex laugh or smile more? These are interesting questions because they exploit a seemingly trivial example of behaviour (humour production/appreciation) in order to provide an explanation of a broader difference in the sexes and why and how they behave and interact. One theory, for example, suggests that the use of humour serves a well-trodden evolutionary purpose to enhance mate selection via competition, and we will return to this later because it may explain one of the most striking, if controversial, findings in the psychology of humour.

The term used to describe a person's ability to generate humour is humour production ability (HPA) and generally describes the ability to produce jokes and funny remarks and to make others laugh. Gill Greengross from the University of Aberystwyth and his colleagues from North Carolina reviewed evidence which sought to answer the question of whether men or women produce more humour and whether one sex is funnier than the other (Greengross, Silvia & Nusbaum,

2020). They undertook a meta-analysis of published and unpublished data and described some of the protocols typically used in experiments on humour production. They note that participants are usually asked to provide their own funny caption to a cartoon or a picture, or they might be asked to provide a funny answer to a riddle or a nonsensical question ("What would have happened if the oceans were full of orange juice?") or participants might be asked to provide an amusing definition for a nonword (rarely are participants asked to draw their response – they are invariably asked to provide a verbal response). The output end (dependent variable) of the experiment also varies – some studies have time restrictions on answering and others allow unlimited time; some studies require only one response per stimulus, others multiple responses. Judges then rate these responses on various dimensions such as funniness, humorousness, enjoyment and so on, usually on some Likert-type line scale where people record a rating from 1 to 7 where 1 is not at all funny, and so on.

The authors examined statistics from 28 studies published between 1976 and 2018. The total number of participants was 5057, 67% of whom were women. They found that when the funniness of the output of men and women was assessed, men's output was judged to be funnier than women's. This result was found regardless of the sex of the paper's author or the person making the judging (the number of men and women judges was almost identical). The output restriction did moderate this result. The positive funniness judgement for men was especially salient if participants were required to make one, rather than multiple, responses. Other (non-significant) findings that were noteworthy included no effect of time – the results were consistent across the 40 years, although there are few studies pre-2000 – and no effect of culture or type of sample (student vs. non-student). The obvious question, then, is why was men's humour perceived as funnier?

COMEDY, HUMOUR AND ATTRACTION

One theory tries to account for this from an evolutionary/mate selection perspective. Sexual selection theory determines that sex differences in mating strategies have evolved to maximise survival and minimise potential costs. Because women's parental investment is greater than men's, they may select traits in a male partner which they regard as being valuable in a long-term mate and which signifies mental fitness (this is the mental fitness indicator theory proposed by Miller in 2000, 2007). Some have argued that activities such as language, arts, sports and humour have evolved as mating strategies to make men/women more attractive to each other (we will address how broadly this applies later; much of this theory is based on heterosexual attraction/mate selection). Humour therefore becomes a fitness indicator, and the assumption is that funnier men are more attractive to women and that men will generate more humour in order to attract a mate and engage in a competitive strategy of mate attraction using humour. Evolutionary pressure compels men to be funnier because they are competing against other funny men who may be of similar age, build, musculature and health and have similar physical resources. If humour is a fitness indicator, women should more attracted to funny/funnier men. (An alternative evolutionary explanation is that we engage in humour to attract and engage in social relationships which is a plausible explanatory mechanism for the use of humour in non-sexual/mating contexts in which strangers interact; Li et al., 2009).

Is this true? The evidence suggests that it is. There is cross-cultural research indicating that having a sense of humour is deemed to be more desirable by women in men than by men in women (e.g., Buss, 1988); this is not always found, but it is a more common finding than no difference or the opposite result (men deeming a sense of humour in women to be more important than women do in men). Bressler and Balshine (2006) found that both sexes valued having a good sense of humour in their partner but that women preferred men with high humour production ability, while men preferred women who would appreciate their humour production abilities (they loved an audience and the adulation). An analysis of 101 methods of attracting a mate found that both men and women rated showing a good sense of humour to be the most effective (Buss, 1988), and being humorous is considered an important trait to have in men and women (Feingold, 1992). Some have argued that humour is one way of managing long-term relationships, such as marriage, and studies suggest that those in the most satisfying marriages are the ones with humorous spouses (Hall, 2017, 2019), and frequency of humour use is correlated with relationship satisfaction (Campbell & Moroz, 2014). On the basis that we are attracted to people that are similar to us – the homophily theory of interpersonal attraction – some have argued that the sharing of humour and the exchange of laughter between two people would likely result in an increase in perceived intimacy (Fraley & Aron, 2004), and there is some evidence that married couples are more alike in terms of their humour (Priest & Thein, 2003), although there is not much research available in this area and some research does not support this.

Satisfaction with a relationship is reported to increase when one spouse uses positive humour and decreases if a spouse uses negative humour (Butzer & Kuiper, 2008; Hall, 2019). One study found that positive humour helped bring couples closer together by resolving conflict (Cann, Davis & Zapata, 2011). Cann et al., however, found no similarity in humour styles between spouses, and Saroglou, Lacour and Demeure's (2010) study of 146 couples found that aggressive, "earthy" and self-defeating (negative) humour use was correlated between spouses but affiliative and self-enhancing (positive) humour was not. A similar study, which also examined couples who had been married for 10 years or more, did find that one spouse's humour style was correlated with the other's (Hahn & Campbell, 2016). In a sample of 239 Taiwanese married couples who had been betrothed for at least 10 years, Tsai, Wu, Chang and Chen (2019) found that the husbands were more likely to show aggressive or self-defeating humour than were the wives and that these predicted the other's behaviour (humour style). Generally, however, the study found that the couples had similar humour styles.

Sex differences in preferences for a person with a sense of humour are also found in studies of lonely-hearts ads and online dating profiles. Men are more likely than women to advertise their sense of humour and how funny they are in adverts and are more likely to make attempts at humour. Women are twice as likely to seek a partner who displays humour plumage than are men and are more likely to want a partner who makes them laugh. Men do not routinely set this as a requirement or desire: adverts by men which feature humour are regarded as more attractive by women, but women's use of humour in ads does not significantly affect men's desire. Greengross and Miller (2011) found that individuals who scored high in humour production ability were more successful sexually and romantically, having more sexual partners, having sex for the first time earlier and having more sexual encounters than those who scored low on HPA. A vignette study in which undergraduates judged the profiles of people who had a good, average or no sense of humour found that the individuals with the good sense of humour were regarded as more suitable and likely romantic partners than were those with average or no sense of humour (McGee & Shevlin, 2009). In an unusual conclusion, one study noted that women with humorous partners had stronger and more frequent orgasms (Gallup, Ampel, Wedberg & Pogosjan, 2014), a correlation that is probably stronger than any sense of causation.

When people flirt, they laugh more, smile more, make greater eye contact and touch more, although the literature on flirting is surprisingly limited (Apostolou & Christoforou, 2020). One study found that eye contact followed by smiling by a female confederate led to an approach rate of 60% by male participants in a bar (Walsh & Hewitt, 1985). There are also sex differences: men think that flirting which suggests sexual access is more effective, while women find flirting to be more effective if it suggests exclusivity, caring and commitment (Wade & Feldman, 2016). In a study of 808 participants from Greece and Cyprus, Apostolou and Christoforou asked people to write down some of the positive things they experienced during flirting which made them want to act on the flirting. The top trait (of 47 identified) was humour, as you can see in Table 3.1.

Table 3.1 The most positive traits which people say facilitate flirting

Trait	Frequency appearing in participants' responses
Humour	216
Intelligence	117
Good looks	97
Politeness	90
Honesty	54
Intense interest in me	48
Good with words	42
Persistence	37
Respect	36

(The less relevant/important traits – the bottom of the 47 – were cheerfulness, maturity, having a nice smell, seriousness and having unusual hobbies.)

Men and women, if asked to indicate which sex is funnier, give men as the answer – not that women are not judged funnier; the judgement was not an absolute but a relative evaluation that men are funnier (Nevo, Nevo & Yin, 2001). In one study, the percentages agreeing were 94% (men) and 89% (women) (Mickes, Walker, Parris, Mankoff & Christenfeld, 2012), although this was a study with only 32 participants. Hooper, Sharpe and Roberts (2016) found that 62% of their participants regarded men as having greater HPA, 34% thought that the sexes were about equal and 4% regarded women as being the funnier. Furthermore, when the sex of a humorous work is concealed, funny captions and cartoons are more often attributed to men than to women (Mickes et al., 2012). People who regard themselves as more masculine are more likely to report using humour more in romantic relationships to attract a mate (Ross & Hall, in press), and men regarded their HPA to be better and greater than that of their competitors. Women who were less likely to make the first move in a relationship were those less likely to use humour as an attractant. Women prefer men with a high HPA, and men prefer women who laugh at their jokes and their attempts at humour (Hone, Hurwitz & Lieberman, 2015).

Of course, as noted earlier, this analysis and analyses like it are focused exclusively on heterosexual relationships and whether HPA is relevant to mate choice in opposite-sex couples. There is hardly any research which has examined the importance or otherwise of HPA to homosexual male and female or nonbinary couples. Would the same pattern emerge in same-sex couples where one individual would adopt the stereotypical "male" role and the other the stereotypical "female" role?

INTELLIGENCE AND HUMOUR

Tied to the concept of mental fitness is intelligence. Evolutionary psychology argues that competition and parental investment will mean that a woman will be attracted to a partner who is (1) supportive, (2) able to care for their partner and offspring by providing physical and emotional resources and (3) intelligent, and this is linked to the other two. A brighter male should bring accompanying long-term benefits. There seems to be a link between intelligence and humour, particularly between verbal intelligence and humour. For example, general intelligence and having a good sense of humour are positively correlated (Howrigan & MacDonald, 2008). Humour has also been associated with status (in men), with shows of humour are allied with perceived respect and esteem (Bitterly, Brooks & Schweitzer, 2017), perhaps because the use of humour signals confidence.

To examine this relationship explicitly, Greengross and Miller (2011) asked 400 undergraduates to complete a non-verbal intelligence task, a vocabulary task, a humour generation task (providing captions for pictures) and a mating success survey. They found that general and verbal intelligence predicted humour generation which, in turn, predicted mating success. That is, the more intelligent participants were more likely to produce humour and were more likely to have had more sexual partners. Spouses, however, are less likely to consider their partners' intelligence to be as important as kindness, dependability and understanding, even though they appreciate having a good sense of humour. For example, Weisfeld et al. (2011) asked 411 Chinese, 405 Russian, 453 Turkish, 419 North American and 1336 British couples (i.e., 3024 married couples) to complete a marital satisfaction questionnaire and to answer the question: "How often does your spouse make you laugh?" All cultures, except Russia, had couples where the husbands were perceived to make wives laugh more than wives made husbands laugh. In the Russian sample, the wives were regarded as funnier. This ability to make partners/spouses laugh was associated with marital satisfaction across all cultures and was especially associated with the satisfaction of wives.

Are intelligent people more likely to produce more comedy? Christensen et al. (2018) administered a series of cognitive ability tests to 270 young adults who were also asked to generate comic responses to stimuli. All three of the tests – especially the test of general intelligence – predicted humour production: the higher the score, the greater the production.

Curiously, in studies where women judge the desirability of men who use humour, those men who do use humour are judged to be more desirable and socially adept but are also judged to be less intelligent (and trustworthy) than those who generate less humour (Bressler & Balshine, 2006).

DO MEN AND WOMEN LAUGH AT THE SAME THINGS?

Marti Caine commenting on "dirty comedy" once said:

> I love it, cos it makes me laugh, and if it makes me laugh it's a tonic, and I don't care, cos I'm not prudish and I'm not narrow minded and anything that pertains to life has got to be funny . . . it's a natural cleansing process – bringing out sex into the open. Words are just words.

Words, obviously, mean a lot in comedy, and some words are perceived as being very offensive. At the one end of offence, you have the lubricious, ribald sweariness of a Lenny Bruce, Bette Midler or Jerry Sadowitz, and at the other you have the comedy that provokes and alienates because of its racism and its sexism (such as the acts of Bernard Manning and Dapper Laughs). One of the filthiest jokes in comedy is "*The Aristocrats*", a joke so famous an entire film was made about it.

The types of comedy men and women laugh at are actually quite similar, although some early studies indicated that men had preferences for (laughed more at) certain types of humour (sexual humour, in particular), and there continues to be discussion regarding whether men and women respond similarly to sexist humour.

There are preferences in terms of film genre, with women tending to prefer romantic or melodramatic films more than do men (Harris et al., 2000). Men tend to prefer violent content in spy movies, war movies, Westerns and cartoons (Blanchard, Graczyk & Blanchard, 1986) and express more pleasure towards these. Another study (Wühr, Lange & Schwarz, 2017) found that men preferred action, adventure, erotic, fantasy, historical, horror, sci-fi, thriller, war and Western films; women preferred animation, comedy, drama, heimat, and romantic films. Both sexes liked crime and mystery equally (see Martin, 2019 for a review). A study of preferences for different types of comic adverts found that men and women found comic wit funnier than they did sentimental comedy, but men evaluated satire more positively than did women; women preferred sentimental comedy more than did men (Schwarz, Hoffmann & Hutter, 2015). Dara Greenwood (2010) found that people who were made sad preferred dark comedy or a social drama and people who were made to feel happy preferred slapstick comedy or action adventure. Women expressed a preference for romantic genres, with men preferring action, suspense and dark comedy. Sad men, in particular, preferred dark comedies.

One early study of male and female comics found that women comics were more likely to disparage themselves than were men (Levine, 1976). Self-deprecation was observed in around two-thirds of the women's routines but in about a tenth of the men's. With the caveat that some of the stimuli employed in early (and, in fairness, some later) studies are of questionable comedic content, some studies found no differences between male and female UK undergraduate students in terms of their response to female-dominated, male-dominated, sexual, disparaging or nonsense humour. On the other hand, a large number of historical studies reported two findings: that men enjoyed jokes/cartoons that disparaged women rather than men and that women also expressed the same response, if there was any difference between the sexes at all. Some studies also found that women enjoyed jokes where the object of disparagement was a man, and others found that men found sexual humour funny regardless of the sex of the object (e.g., La Fave, 1972; Cantor, 1976, amongst many others). Building on this research, Butland and Ivy (1990) found no such effect (men did not prefer jokes disparaging women and neither did women), but they did note a difference for one type of joke when they categorised their sample into traditional men and women: traditional males did enjoy the joke disparaging women more. Women didn't.

In 2001 Barbara Henkin and Jefferson Fish took early studies to task for employing materials created by men (not an especially strong criticism), depicting a male viewpoint (a valid criticism) and being sexual or aggressive in nature – and women are the object in both types. They also reasonably point out that it is often not the membership group that is important (sex, in this case), but the reference group (who we ally ourselves with). Despite a literature showing that women enjoyed "female-oriented" sexist humour more than did men and that women also enjoyed aggressive and sexual humour in which the object was a woman, Henkin and Fish did not replicate these findings in a sample of 120 undergraduates from the United States who rated sexual and aggressive cartoons (the object's sex was swapped in the jokes). Love and Deckers (1989) explored undergraduate men's and women's responses to sexual, sexist and aggressive cartoons, finding that for women only sexist cartoons correlated with funniness – the more sexist the cartoons, the less funny they were – and for men, only sex-themed cartoons correlated with funniness – the greater the sex content, the funnier the cartoon.

There is also evidence that the more sexist a person's beliefs, the more likely he or she is to find sexist humour funny. Disparaging humour is usually a form of expressing a socially unacceptable point of view or providing a channel for expressing some form of prejudice that might be generally accepted; in short, to disparage an outgroup thereby enhancing the in-group. Sexist and aggressive humour achieves this. People who make jokes about people from a specific region of their country are more likely to hold negative, stereotypical views of that region's burghers (Maio et al., 1997; Gallois & Callan, 1985). Other examples include studies in which exposure to sexist comedy sketches have been associated with stereotyped-based judgements about men and women at a later date and that white participants were more likely to hold negative views about black people if they were exposed to disparaging humour about black people (Ford, 1997). These are examples of priming or stereotype activation.

However, as Ford, Richardson and Petit (2015) acknowledge, these studies did not include a non-humorous control condition. One study which did introduce a non-humorous disparagement condition did not find that exposure to disparaging humour affected people's attitudes consistently (Olson et al., 1999). Ford (2000) found that pre-existing sexist beliefs made people who were exposed to sexist humour (compared with non-sexist humour or neutral material) more accepting of sex discrimination. These results were similar to those of Ryan and Kanjorski (1998), who found that men enjoyed jokes disparaging women more but those men who endorsed rape-related beliefs were likely to enjoy them even more.

In Ford's study, when the participants were asked to examine the sexist humour critically (they were asked how offensive it was and how critical they were of the behaviour in the humour), the effects of the sexist humour reported in the earlier experiment were not observed. People with pro-feminist views and more liberal views were also less likely to find sexist cartoons funny (Henkin & Fish, 1986; Moore, Griffiths & Payne, 1987). Consistent with Ford, Greenwood and Isbell (2002) found that men and women who were described as high hostile sexists were more likely to find dumb blonde jokes funnier and less offensive after they had listened to a conversation between two men in which one man complained about his girlfriend and implied she was a dumb blonde.

A similar result was reported by Thomas and Esses (2004). They found that high hostile sexists were more likely to repeat jokes in which women were disparaged and were more likely to find those jokes funny than did less hostile men. Funniness mediated the relationship: the jokes had to be judged as funny in order for them to be repeated. In a very practical example of what might occur if people are exposed to tendentious humorous material, Ford, Boxer, Armstrong and Edel (2008) found that undergraduates who were hostile sexists were less likely to donate to a women's charity after reading sexist jokes. They also found that those participants were more likely to cut the budget of a women's organisation (but not other student organisations) after exposure to sexist comedy video clips but not neutral ones. In a related experiment in which men were asked to imagine themselves as managers who had made a sexist remark to a new woman employee, those who were high hostile sexists felt less shame and guilt about the remark after reading sexist than neutral jokes or non-humorous material (Ford, Wentzel & Lorion, 2001).

In terms of differences between men and women, there are two consistent findings and one is more controversial than the other (that men are funnier). The literature on personality, described next, also throws up some interesting consistencies but also its fair share of heterogeneity.

HUMOUR STYLES AND PERSONALITY

There have been a few studies of the association between humour styles and personality traits, including two meta-analyses. One empirical study examined the relationship between happiness, humour styles, extraversion, self-esteem and optimism and found that happiness was positively correlated with affiliative and self-enhancing humour styles and negatively with self-defeating and aggressive styles

(Ford, Lappi & Holden, 2016). The happier people were also more extravert, optimistic and had higher locus of control and self-esteem.

A meta-analysis of 15 studies published in 2015 found that the affiliative humour style was positively associated with extraversion; that self-enhancing humour was positively related to agreeableness, openness to experience and conscientiousness; and that neuroticism was positively associated with self-defeating humour (those using this style were more likely to be neurotic) and negatively associated with self-enhancing humour (more neurotic people would use this style less) (Mendiburo-Seguel, Páez & Martínez-Sánchez, 2015). These results are what the authors describe as homogenous – that is, they are strongly seen across studies rather than shown strongly within a portion of the studies. A strong correlation in a third of studies might create an overall positive correlation across all studies, but this would not demonstrate that the effect was genuine and "homogeneous".

The most recent meta-analysis, of 24 studies and 11,791 partic-ipants across 13 countries, found similar results to the 2015 study (Plessen et al., 2020). Self-enhancing and affiliative styles were positively associated with extraversion, agreeableness, openness to experience and conscientiousness and negatively associated with neuroticism, whereas aggressive and self-defeating styles were posi-tively associated with neuroticism and negatively related to agreeable-ness and conscientiousness. They argue that the results demonstrate the importance of positive humour styles to subjective well-being, although they note that the literature is dominated by Western sam-ples. Culture, as you will see later, has been the subject of some study in comedy and humour, but not much, and the majority of the sam-ples recruited in humour studies is either Western or European.

LOVING/HATING BEING LAUGHED AT

A slightly different taxonomy to the normal humour styles is based on those groups of people who either enjoy laughing at others or who hate being laughed at. These are not personality types per se – they are behavioural dispositions – but they do correlate with some personality traits (even if not always consistently). The German psychologist Wilibald Ruch has driven much of the research in this very specific field and has identified three behavioural types: those who display a fear of being laughed at (gelotophobia), those who enjoy being laughed at (gelotophilia) and those who enjoy laughing at others (katagelastica). Gelotophobes fear the rejection of others (pathologically so) and have been found to be introverted and neurotic (Ruch & Proyer, 2009a) but show no other strong personality traits.

Gelotophobia is seen as a continuum, rather than as a category, and so we can all fall along this continuum somewhere from no fear to extreme fear of being laughed at. People high in gelotophobia were found to be unstable introverts (Proyer & Ruch, 2010) and the relationship satisfaction of those high scorers is also low – gelotophobes are more likely to be single, whereas those who enjoy being laughed at are more likely to have positive romantic partnerships (Brauer & Proyer, 2018). People scoring high in gelotophobia are also more likely to show attachment anxiety and avoidance behaviour and show less likelihood of entering a romantic relationship (Brauer, Proyer & Ruch, 2019). Proyer and Ruch (2009b) also found that gelotophilia was associated with increased extraversion and was more common in men, whereas Brauer et al. found that it was associated with less avoidance behaviour. Katagelastics in Proyer and Ruch's study scored highly for extraversion and psychoticism (and tended to be younger men); Brauer et al. also found that katagelastica was associated reliably with attachment anxiety. The cause of these three dispositions is unknown, although a childhood characterised by teasing is surprisingly not a predictor.

HUMOUR ACROSS AND WITHIN CULTURES

Humour is often regarded as universal – in the sense that it is demonstrated or expressed in different cultures in the world in various ways – but there are some reported differences in (1) the sense of humour expressed by different cultures and (2) the types of comedy enjoyed. The most universal humour is that which is expressed non-verbally. This is why Mr Bean, Benny Hill, Inspector Clouseau and animated films are popular in English- and non-English-speaking countries: the humour relies on slapstick or physical humour (or, if language is used, humour which draws attention to the ridiculousness of the language or the comic's delivery) which is easier to understand and which is less culture-bound. Albanians were famously fond of the beleaguered, maladroit, loveable idiot character played by Norman Wisdom in his films for this reason (as well as the reason that he was one of the few Western actors whose films the country's previous communist dictator allowed on the country's television). When the actor died, the prime minister of the country wrote a letter of condolence to the actor's family.

There is some research on smiling and laughter cross-culturally and whether they are seen consistently across cultures and nations and whether they are perceived as the same. For example, Rychlowska et al.'s (2015) study of emotional expression across nine nations, which included Canada, France, Germany, India, Indonesia, Israel, Japan, New Zealand and the United States, found that those cultures which demonstrated more smiling were likely to be more heterogenous – that is, they have a long history of migration and integration.

A more unusual study linked the degree of smiling to a country's perceived corruption (Krys et al., 2016). Around 5000 participants from 44 cultures were asked to associate smiling and non-smiling faces with various psychological attributes such as stupidity, intelligence, honesty, naturalness and so on. The negative traits were included because the authors note that some of the uses of smiles are not necessarily positive but manipulative: dominance smiles, for example, which are used – as the name suggests – to control other members of the group and reflect scheming or critical attitudes. They also looked at "uncertainty avoidance": societies perceived as low on this tend to perceive the future as being unpredictable and do not know how to respond appropriately; the researchers also examined the degree of corruption present in the societies they studied. They found two things: respondents from low uncertainty avoidance cultures regarded smiling people as less intelligent than non-smiling people; people in highly corrupt societies found smiling faces to be less trustworthy.

There is some recent research on cross-cultural expressions of laughter. One study found that people across cultures (26 societies from six world regions) were able to distinguish above chance whether laughter was shared between friends or strangers (Bryant et al., 2016). The same team also found that people across 21 cultures (including Australia, India, Samoa, Turkey, The Netherlands, the United States, Iran and Peru) could distinguish between spontaneous and volitional laughter – the success rate varied from 56% to 69%, not great, but above chance (Bryant et al., 2018).

There is also some, but not much, research on cultural differences in humour, and most of this was reviewed in our 2013 paper (Martin & Sullivan, 2013). In that study, we administered the Multidimensional Sense of Humour Scale to British, Australian and North American adults and found that British people held more negative views of humorous people than did Australians and that Americans used humour more in social contexts than did British people (men, as expected, produced more humour than did women but production was not affected by culture). Our review of the literature examined what cultural difference, if any, existed up until that point. We found at the broadest level that humour in magazine advertising differed across the United States, China and France and that US TV commercials were more likely to use affiliative, aggressive and self-defeating humour than were Mexican TV commercials, which tended to use self-enhancing humour. Some of the other findings included the following:

- North American respondents preferred aggressive humour more than did Belgian, Senegalese, Chinese or Hong Kong respondents.
- Hungarians found jokes about ethnic stereotypes funnier than did English participants or English-Hungarian bilingual participants.
- A study of Chinese, Israeli and North American students found that Chinese students used aggressive humour more than did the Americans (but used sexual humour less).
- In the same study, Chinese participants were less likely than other groups to use humour as a coping mechanism.

- Lebanese students were less affiliative and self-enhancing than were Canadians and less aggressive than Belgians.
- Participants from the United States, Israel and China generated similar amounts of laughter, smiling and joke-telling; Singaporean students were less likely to use humour as a coping mechanism.
- Americans were more likely to generate humour than were Croatians.

Much has been made of the differences between Eastern and Western cultures, although this segregation of people in an unsophisticated way into geographical lumps is probably not the best way of characterising nations or cultures given the variety of sub-cultures within each. A similar, but more theoretically sound, distinction is made between collectivistic and individualistic cultures. To this end, Hiranandani and Yue (2014) found that Indian and Hong Kong students reported using affiliative and self-enhancing humour more than the two negative humour styles and both of those cultures are described as collectivistic. Hong Kong students, on the other hand, reported using aggressive humour and self-defeating more than did mainland Chinese students (Yue, Hao & Goldman, 2010; Yue, Liu, Jiang & Hiranandani, 2014; Jiang, Lu & Hiranandani, 2016). The East vs. West studies suggest that Easterners are less funny and generate less humour than do Westerners. Chinese and American students both viewed Americans as being funnier than the Chinese (Jiang, Yue & Lu, 2011), and Canadians produced more humour than did the Chinese (Chen & Martin, 2007). Lu, Martin, Usova and Galinsky (2019) point out that the Chinese have a phrase – *hua zhong qu chong* – which is used to berate those who use humour to try and stand out (show off), which suggests that a comedic disposition in Chinese culture is not a positive trait.

IT'S NOT AS FUNNY ANYMORE: HUMOUR AND AGEING

It's not uncommon for our advancing years to be accompanied by not especially positive declines in all sorts of behaviours, echoing

Jaques's Seventh Age of Man in *As You Like It*, "sans eyes, sans teeth, sans everything". Well, not quite everything. When it comes to humour, the evidence suggests that our enjoyment of humour continues – and in fact, increases – as we get older at least until we reach 60, and then it declines (Greengross, 2013). What does decline is our ability to comprehend humour, a finding that is likely attributable to declines in cognitive functions necessary for joke/humour comprehension. The decline may also be responsible for the reduction in humour production as we get older.

Shammi and Stuss (2003), in a study with small samples (17 young people and 20 over-60s), found that the older sample judged humorous and neutral statements to be funnier than did the comparison group, but its ability to complete jokes by choosing the right ending (or choosing the right caption for a cartoon) was poorer. The performance on the joke task correlated with performance on a working memory task and a task of abstract verbal reasoning. The conclusion of this study was that appreciation was not affected in the older group, but comprehension was. A quasi-replication with a slightly larger sample found a similar result – older participants were worse at the joke completion and caption-provision tasks than were the younger participants and were comparatively worse at tests of abstract reasoning, the ability to think flexibly, short-term memory and verbal IQ (Mak & Carpenter, 2007). A much larger study (over 4000 participants aged between 14 and 66 years) found that enjoyment of incongruity resolution jokes increased with age but the appreciation of nonsense humour declined. This study also found that the more conservative the participant, the less likely they were to enjoy nonsense jokes where the resolution of ambiguity was silly. Similar comprehension difficulties in older samples are seen when they try to explain the behaviour of characters in jokes (Uekermann, Channon & Daum, 2006), suggesting that their ability to mentalise (their theory of mind) is declining or is impaired.

Behaviourally, the amount of laughter we produce declines with age, and we particularly laugh less in the evening when we are much older compared to when we are younger (Martin & Kuiper, 1999).

Older women (>60) are especially less expressive, laughing an average of 11.7 times a day compared with 22.7 in women under 24. Older men, on the other hand, laugh more often in the morning than do younger men. Types of humour also seem to differ between younger and older samples, with the older group showing less affiliative humour than younger samples but older women showing more self-enhancing humour than do younger women (Martin et al., 2003). Younger samples tend to show more aggressive humour. One problem with all of these studies is that they are cross-sectional rather than longitudinal, so it is unclear whether they are reporting group differences or age-related differences.

CONCLUSION

If there is one thing we can conclude from the preceding sections, it's that humour research is never straightforward but it is enjoyably unstraightforward. The research on sex differences, personality, humour styles, culture and ageing has all highlighted similarities between the ways groups respond and produce humour, but also specific differences in the way they appreciate, produce or comprehend humour. In the next chapter, we will consider a more specific kind of individual and a more specific individual difference: being a comedian.

4

COMEDIANS AND THEIR PERSONALITIES

Comedians, according to Howard Pollio and John Edgerly, are a "unique class of people whose very actions and behaviour set them apart from everyone else"(Pollio & Edgerly, 1976). A definition which can also apply to terrorists and babies, but the motivations and reasoning of those who choose to make a living from making us laugh seem to be different from those of other professions. "There is one group of people who go out of their way to highlight their own absurdities, weaknesses and ridiculousness and then shout about it for profit and the name of art," writes Robin Ince in his book *I'm a Joke and So Are You*, "Those people are comedians . . . it's as if they are deliberately going out of their way to potentially embarrass themselves" (p. 3). The hoary old cliche that comedians are comedians because they are channelling some previously constipated emotional trauma or neurosis and are expressing their tragedy through comedy is largely a myth (and we will look at this evidence shortly). The television play, *The Comedian*, written by a pre–*Twilight Zone* Rod Sterling starred Mickey Rooney as a deeply unpleasant, venal, scabrous comedian and illustrated another caricature of comedians as being damaged goods, not particularly pleasant to know and people to whom we should give a wide berth.

Many comedians and comics have talked about or written about their mental health and their engagement in psychotherapy: Woody

DOI: 10.4324/9780429347269-4

Allen, Spike Milligan, David Baddiel and John Cleese are some of the more well-known. Cleese has even written highly successful books with the psychiatrist, Robin Skinner, about our relationships with other people. Milligan, reflecting on the Janus-headed nature of comedy, said in an interview that "I suppose I am the way that I am because comedy needs a vast spectrum of emotion. There are no heights unless there are depths". Cleese acknowledged the reluctance of comedians to seek psychological help: "Some performers think that psychiatry would destroy their art. They'll never consider it for fear that sanity would take away what makes them good performers", a reflection also made by Stephen Fry in the context of medication and his bipolar disorder. Larry David, encouraged by his friend and fellow comedian, Richard Lewis (a big supporter of psychotherapy), to attend a therapy session was so horrified by what he saw and heard that he fled his session and hid in a telephone box. When Cleese asked Woody Allen how his 25-year engagement with psychotherapy was going, the American apparently replied: "Slowly".

Despite how popular and successful the profession is, there is very little research on the psychology of the comedian – why they become comedians, why they create the material they do and why they carry on trying to make people laugh. What little research there is has focused on comic performers, rather than writers, artists or cartoonists, and these accounts have been largely anecdotal, if diverting biographical reflections. There are many good examples of these, and one of the more recent is Judd Apatow's *Sick in the Head*, a Brobdignagian collection of interviews with some well-known comedians and comedy performers. Apatow himself, of course, is no comedy slacker, having written *Bridesmaids, Freaks and Geeks, Anchorman, Knocked Up* and *The 40-Year Old Virgin*, amongst others, and helped develop *Girls* with Lena Denham.

One observation Apatow makes and which he thinks has traction throughout all of his interviewees is that "these people were part of a tribe – the tribe of comedians . . . my whole life I'd wanted friends who had similar interests. . . . It was lovely having this interest that no one shared" (p. xiv), a feeling, a form of competitive camaraderie that is echoed in many stand-up comedians' dressing rooms and holding areas in between the stage anxiety and bowel disorders.

Apatow's own early exposure and motivation to do comedy are also reflected in the childhood behaviour of other comedians. Jerry Seinfeld used to record *Saturday Night Live* with an audio tape recorder; Jimmy Fallon used to tape each one of the shows. Amy Schumer watched and listened to Letterman, Carlin, Pryor, Rita Rudner and The Muppets. Robin Ince recounts enthusiastically taping comedy shows from the television, as did *The Thick of It*, *Avenue 5*, *Breeders* and *Veep* writer, Simon Blackwell. The peerless Garry Shandling became obsessed with comedy at the age of 10 but did not see a real club comedian (Carlin, again) until he was 20. In conversation with Apatow, he said: "All comedians and comedy writers I know all pretended like they had radio shows, talking into their tape recorders".

This entertainment ethic is often reflected in a work ethic – writing as much down as possible, the notebook by the bed, the wanting to make people laugh. Seinfeld again:

> I do it compulsively. I have a big, yellow legal pad. And once I get that pad open, I can't stop. It's kind of like free-diving. You have a certain amount of air and then you just have to come up. I'm good for an hour or two and then I collapse on the couch and sleep. . . . This is one of the perils of the job, You can work yourself to destruction. Because the work is interesting and exciting and all these opportunities are rare and wonderful and hard to resist.

Jon Stewart has made similar observations: "With stand-up, you're never done. You always feel like you've got to keep that notebook by the bed. And so you stop experiencing anything. You just exist purely as an observer. . . . It's exhausting". Speaking of writing *Young Frankenstein* with Marty Feldman, Mel Brooks "never stopped writing. We wrote, rewrote, rewrote, rewrote, rewrote. Someone once said you never finish anything, you just abandon it. We abandoned *Young Frankenstein*".

This early experience of, and appetite for, comedy may be part of what makes a great comedian rare. Seinfeld himself noted in the interview with Apatow that "there will be only a very few great comedians because comedy itself is so difficult. No matter how many people do it, it's just a rare combination of skills and talents that go into making a great comedian". Terry Jones made a similar point to highlight how hard comedy is. Bad comedy, he says, makes people very angry. You don't find that sort of reaction to bad tragedy, only comedy. Stebbins (1980) argued that "using humour is like driving on a poorly maintained road; one does so at one's own risk. A practical joke may be carried off with the hope of generating amiability, but be defined by the subject as an aggressive, irritating act" (p. 94).

Comedians, fools and clowns have appeared through history for centuries, and some have elevated the status of the comedian to heights that are inappropriately stratospheric. Welsford (1935), for example, argued that fools exist not because "the fool is a creator of beauty but of . . . freedom". His abuse at the hands of others demonstrates his (and at that time, it was usually a he) resilience and stoicism. Others ascribed to clowns an almost quasi-religious role: Pollio and Edgerly cite Klapp (1972), who argued that the fool or clown should be regarded as possessing the same status as the hero or villain, which in literature he justifiably could. There are all manner of psychoanalytic interpretations of the meaning of clowns, such as their being a Jungian archetype prepared to re-unite a society with matters it has long since repressed. Like most psychoanalytic interpretations, it has the depth and rigour of bubble wrap but, until very recently, these were the characterisation of clowns and comedians that were, if not dominant, then certainly not uncommon.

More recently, a small cornucopia of books has been published which has examined comedians' view of their work, their motivation and how they create the work that they do. Most of these include interviews with the leading comedians or comic writers of the day or those with a cherished and well-regarded hinterland and are worth seeking out. They include Bruce Dessau's *Beyond a Joke* (2012), David Bradbury and Joe McGrath's *Now That's Funny* (1998), Jim Driver's *Funny*

Talk (1995), William Cook's *Ha Bloody Ha* (1994), John Hind's *The Comic Inquisition* (1991), Oliver Double's *Stand-Up!* (1997), Mike Sacks's *Poking a Dead Frog* (2014) and Judd Apatow's *Sick in the Head* (2015) which we discussed earlier.

Some of the earliest empirical work – and the word empirical may be doing some heavy lifting here – was conducted by Pollio and his colleagues who wanted to discover whether there were clusters or types of comedians (Pollio, Edgerly & Jordan, 1972). They asked students to come up with as many names of comedians as they could, then a list of 37 names was presented to another group, which was asked to identify a comedian who was similar to each of the names listed. Pollio et al. identified eight factors (e.g., "comediennes", "black comedians", "talk-show/verbal" performers and others). The seemingly irrelevant exercise was transformed into a more meaningful one when they began to discriminate generic patterns in the responses. For example, the researchers argued that the students' classification divided comedians along two broad categories: "shallow" and "style properties", where shallow properties described the comedians' colour or sex or medium of working and style described verbal felicity and use of aggressive or hostile humour. They then asked students to associate adjectives with the comedians. The results were, well, not positive ("we were absolutely amazed by the sheer quantity of unpleasant, or negative adjectives such as fat, nasty, gross, clumsy, stupid and deformed", p. 250). Fifty-three per cent of the adjectives were negative in nature, 34% were positive. "Fat", "old" and "nasty" were commonly used. Comedians seemed to bring out the worst, and the most brutally descriptive, in people.

Probably the first study of the type of pathway comics and comedians take to reach their vocation was that of Fisher and Fisher (1981) in their book *Pretend the World Is Funny and Forever: A Psychological Analysis of Comedians, Clowns and Actors*. They examined the personal histories of 43 professional comics'/clowns' and 41 professional actors' personal histories to identify historical predictors of professional creative choice. They found that few comedians chose comedy as a vocation, but entered it gradually, as a way of whittling and honing a craft (clowns, on the other hand, had a clearer career trajectory – in half of a sample of 15 clowns studied, the father had been a clown and the families were circus families).

One factor which did emerge from the study was that a large number of comics came from families of lower socio-economic status, a finding which had also been reported over 20 years before. The comedians in Fisher and Fisher's study were identified as being the class clowns and not among the highest academic achievers. Their parents provided little support for their comedic ambitions, and this lack of support resulted in some bitterness experienced later in life. The Fishers concluded that a leitmotif among their comedians was the notion of evil versus virtue, that the comedy was intended to heal or to change and that they made the best fist of portraying themselves as being not bad: "He is alternately the Devil, the Angel, and an Antichrist who denies that any meaningful standards about evil and virtue are possible" (p. 70). Admittedly, this conclusion was based on the responses to the Rorschach test.

Their interview data, however, pointed to a different perspective on their participants' motivation to become a comedian. They found that the professional comedians were more likely to have had positions of responsibility in the family when they were growing up: to earn money, to look after others, to look after family members – in short, to grow up quickly. They also found that the comedians had more positive views towards their fathers than their mothers.

The notion of comedy coming from pain, a widely acknowledged cliche in comedy, is nonetheless expressed often by comedians: Garry Shandling, Harold Ramis and Bill Murray all reflect this. "Comedy" says Ramis, "gives them [comedians] a place to work out ideas and emotions but they want you to know how they feel". It's a vulnerability that seems toxically illogical. Comedians, by and large, want to be loved. And it is a profession where rejection is as common as oxygen. Roseanne Barr summed up just this paradox: "you become a comedian because, on some level, you're so insecure that you need people's approval. And then you get yourself in a position where you can get an enormous amount of disapproval but it's worth the risk". Sarah Silverman has said something very similar – that comedy (swearing in particular) gave her a sense of control of her own life: "It became this source of power in a totally peerless life". The need to please is common. Jimmy Fallon said that "I always wanted to please everybody. I always wanted to make everybody proud of me and happy", and Apatow remarked that "I feel shame at the need to make people happy in order to feel good". Lena Dunham said that her comedy, like the comedy of many other sharp comedians, exists to make a point and often a point that does not get made that often:

> People are always telling you that your experience doesn't matter, that it's navel-gazing and unnecessary. "We don't want to hear about 20-something girls who feel like they're 10 pounds over-weight". But we do need to hear it because that's who so many people are. It can be the difference between someone feeling like they have a place in the world and someone feeling they don't.

Harry Shearer has a slightly different perspective: "the reason why people are comedians is to have control over why people laugh at you", a view that is echoed by Roseanne Barr when she says: "my humour comes from wanting to disarm people before they hit me" (this came from Barr's literal family experience – if she made her family laugh, they didn't hit her).

Apatow commenting on the same theme has said that when people laugh at his stand-up he doesn't know if the audience likes him but he knows that they don't dislike him. The joy of an uninhibited audience response, where the comedian's performance is unanimously and positively reinforced, was summed up brilliantly by Stephen Colbert: "if a thousand people are laughing, that sounds like a lot of people. That sounds like bacon frying." Comedians are hungry for bacon frying.

Whether there is a "comic" type – a certain type of individual with a consistent set of traits that defines them as a comedian – is a question to which the answer is probably no. Fisher and Fisher's study found a heterogeneity of personality traits and dispositions in their study of comedians. An early (doctoral) study (Salameh, 1980) which administered a specific personality inventory to 20 stand-up comedians and a control group found that the comedians were more dominant, socially ambitious, aggressive, self-confident, impulsive, outspoken, self-centred and verbally fluent. A study of 21 Israeli comedians reported that writers were above average in intelligence, while performers scored slightly lower (Ziv, 1984). The comedians were introverted, serious and emotionally unstable. Amateur humourists were more stable and extraverted.

More recent studies, adopting more reliable and valid measures, have highlighted significant personality differences between stand-up comedians, amateur comedians, humour writers and college students (Greengross & Miller, 2009). When these groups were studied for their Big Five personality traits (Openness to Experience, Conscientiousness, Extraversion, Agreeableness and Neuroticism), little significant difference was found between the amateurs and the professionals, but there were differences between the comedians and the students: they were more open to experience, but less conscientious, extraverted and agreeable. Humour writers showed greater openness, extraversion, and conscientiousness than did the comedians.

The lack of agreeableness in the comedians was also echoed in another large online study of comedians' personality. Ando, Claridge and Clark (2014) administered a fairly obscure personality scale which measured four dimensions of psychoticism to 500 comedians and 250 actors (the control group), finding that the comedians were significantly more likely to score high on the scale measuring unsociability and depressiveness but also on a scale measuring impulsiveness and manic activity. The authors go on to make some generalisations regarding the group's mental health, which are largely baseless and shouldn't detain us here. It was a study with a large sample, however. It is a pity that it was not put to better use.

Do comedians live longer than the rest of us?

Alfred E. Newman, the ephelidic, jug-eared, gap-toothed cover star of almost every *MAD* magazine ever, observed: "He who laughs, lasts". A tiny little cottage industry of research exists which has tested the metaphorical adage: he who laughs last laughs longest. The earliest systematic study of this was published in 1992 by James Rotton. He examined the age at death and the longevity of 88 living entertainers, 43 dead comedians and a matched sample of non-comic entertainers, 91 humourists and a matched group of non-comic writers. Rotton found that there was no advantage of being a comedian or a funny writer to longevity – they did not live longer than other entertainers. A slightly more direct study – called starkly, "Does Comedy Kill?" – conducted a retrospective analysis of 53 male comedians born between 1900 and 1954 (Stewart & Thompson, 2015). A group of raters was asked to judge the funniness of each. There was no relationship between decade of birth and longevity, but the researchers did find that those comedians judged to be the funniest were those who died soonest. If the comedian was in a team of comedians, the comedian in the team judged to be the funnier was three times more likely to die than was the less funny partner. The results, the authors conclude, suggest that elite comedians are at "increased risk of premature death", but this conclusion is, well, a little premature because this was one small retrospective study with no comparison groups. They did, however, find a similar result in their 2016 study of 200 stand-up comedians, 113 comedy actors and 184 dramatic actors (Stewart, Wiley, McDermott & Thompson, 2016). A study of comedians identified via Wikipedia (1408 of them) found that they were born at around 1915, lived 5 to 10 years longer than non-comedians and were well-educated (Kirkegaard, 2017).

CLOWNING AND THE CLASS CLOWN

The BBC TV sketch series, *The Fast Show*, featured a particularly irritating office companion, Colin Hunt. Hunt was garishly shirted and clownishly coiffed and conducted his entire office interaction via the medium of bad jokes, bad puns and bad physical comedy. That was the joke. His office mate, Pam, was a willing, indulgent and receptive foil. But almost every other visitor and colleague found him as funny as the papilloma virus.

Clowns, generally, are regarded as the broadest of the comic practitioners; they can't not be with their dyed curly wigs, their red noses, painted red mouths, squirty flowers, honking horns and cars that fall to pieces. They reflect a child's version of slapstick, although some children do express intense fear of clowns, especially "evil clowns", a condition termed coulrophobia. The essence of pantomime, which is the embodiment of the clown, saw its apogee in Joseph Grimaldi, the greatest British clown, who practiced and performed in the 19th century. The principal characteristic of pantomime and clowning – apart from the comedy – is its linguistic silence: all is visual or auditory, hardly ever verbal. And this has many comedic advantages, the easy translation across cultures being one. From Charlie Chaplin and Buster Keaton to Benny Hill, Mr Bean and *You've Been Framed*, physical comedy travels and is the comic lingua franca of the world (ditto cartoons), as we saw earlier. Despite its ostensibly frivolous mien, clowning is an act and a practice that is taken quite seriously and by some seriously funny people. The French clown Phillipe Gaulier, for example, who teaches his own Ecole, has been lauded by comedy technicians such as Sasha Baron-Cohen as "the greatest living teacher of clown and modern theatre . . . the funniest man I have ever met". Which brings us back, more prosaically, to Colin Hunt.

Hunt is an example of what in the comedy literature is known as the "organisational fool" – the employee who is more likely than any other to engage in banter, badinage, practical jokes, pranks and endless japery. There are other, less broad, more subtle uses of humour by employees in organisations, and these may help in enabling a discussion of difficult topics that would otherwise remain undiscussed (such as bad management, corruption and other malpractice). The organisational fool has a scholastic analogue in the class clown, and there is a small, but revealing, literature on the characteristics of the class clown – the classmate who makes other classmates laugh and who engages more often than others in telling jokes. Teachers regard class clowns as disruptive, if likeable, and as requiring discipline, but their peers regard them more positively. Conan O' Brien had this to say about the class clown:

> I was not the class clown . . . I've always maintained that the class clown, the guy who when the teacher is out of the room sets the clock back, makes noise, those kids . . . grow up and they're killed in motel shoot-out.

However, the picture is more complicated than this and rarely, if ever, involves a shoot-out.

The earliest systematic study of class clowns was published in 1978 by Damico and Purkey. They surveyed a sample of 3500 eighth-grade children and were able to identify 96 class clowns, nominated by peers, from this group. Compared with 237 non-clowns (identified by teachers), the clowns were more likely to be boys and were regarded by teachers as being more assertive, unruly, attention-seeking, cheerful and to show leadership. They were regarded as accomplishing less. The clowns held less positive attitudes towards their teachers and head teacher. How the class clowns were so designated was fairly arbitrary. Students who received 10 nominations were classed as clowns and those receiving 25 or more were classed as "super class clowns". The percentage of clowns in a class has ranged from 3% (Damico and Purkey's study) to 21% (Priest & Swain, 2002). The authors liken the adolescent clowns to adult wits who are also characterised as being male, assertive, creative and holding positive views of themselves. The reasons for humorous incidents in the classroom and especially those directed toward teachers include a need to be rebellious and for testing the limits of expression but also a motivation to lighten the class atmosphere (Meeus & Mahieu, 2009).

In the largest study of class clowns since Damico and Purkey's study, Wilibald Ruch and his group examined the incidence, correlates and motivations of class clowning in a group of 672 Swiss children and adolescents (Ruch, Platt & Hofmann, 2014). They explored different aspects of class clowning and the "character strength" of class clowns, as well as investigating clowns' levels of happiness and life satisfaction (Ruch et al., 2014, had reported a correlation between humour production and life satisfaction in adolescents). Around 60% of the sample were girls, and the total group mean age was 14.87 years (with a range of 10 to 18). The children completed Platt's Class Clown Behaviour Survey (CCBS) – an 18-item questionnaire that measures class clowning – amongst other measures. The CCBS yields four factors or types,: "identified as class clown", "comic talent", "disruptive rule breaker" and "subversive joker". This and teachers' nominations were used to classify the clowns. Most of the clowns, as the 1978 study found, were boys. Despite being the smaller group, they composed 56% of class clowns.

Clowns were more likely to be less prudent than non-clowns but expressed greater life satisfaction. Male clowns scored higher on all the CCBS factors apart from comic talent, where the sex distribution was more equal. Younger children were more likely than older to identify themselves as class clown. Clowns were more likely to view themselves as high in humour and leadership but low in love of learning. There are limitations to the study, as the authors admit, such as the study providing a snapshot (and of a specific culture) rather than a developmental account of class clowning (Does it stop? Does it continue? One study has examined this, to some degree; see later) and the nature of the classroom and subject was not considered: Is clowning more likely in some disciplines' classes, and are some disciplines' teachers more or less likely to identify children as clowns?

Similar results were found in Wagner's (2019) study of 300 Swiss children (mean age, 13 years). She was interested in the relationship between class clowning and the children's social relationships and functioning and used the Revised Class Play questionnaire to examine this. This measure has been found to predict academic, social and job success up to 10 years after its administration (Gest, Sesma, Masten & Tellegen, 2006); students who are accepted/well-liked tend also to be regarded as helpful, communicative and good leaders. It focuses on four areas: popular leadership (e.g., Does the person make friends easily? Is the person listened to?), prosocial behaviour (good manners with peers), sensitive-isolated (withdrawal behaviour and lack of interaction with others) and aggressive-disrupted (being disruptive in groups). Seventeen teachers rated the children, and Wagner found that children described as class clowns were more popular among teachers and students – they were better liked and had more friends. The comic talent factor of the CCBS was the best predictor of this positive social status – those who were quick witted and liked to make their friends laugh were better liked – and it also predicted the leadership factor of the Revised Class Play questionnaire. The greater the expression of humour in the classroom, the greater the perception of leadership. Clowning was also associated with being more disruptive and less prosocial. The disruptive rule-breaker element of the CCBS was most strongly correlated with aggressive/disruptive behaviour. These clowns mock teachers and the school and are perceived as being impolite and not helpful. In summary, clowning was associated with a mixed bag of outcomes, from positive to negative.

CONCLUSION

This chapter explored a specific type of comedy personality: the comedian and the clown. The next two chapters consider an even more complex set of circumstances: the way in which humour can be used to influence and change behaviour, and not physical behaviour such as laughing or smiling, but behaviour such as health, cognition, memory, message perception, consumption and learning.

5

THE USES OF COMEDY I: HEALTH AND THERAPY

HUMOUR AND PSYCHOLOGICAL WELL-BEING

One of the most distinctive, if inane, exhortations you will be likely to read in a self-help book about the "healing power of laughter" goes something like this: "run without fun and your stride will falter!" The advice, for those who might regard running with fun as being as life-enhancing as racing with ricin, sounds glib − and it is − but the idea behind this is that unless you adopt a humorous joyfulness in your life, you won't enjoy that life as much and you will experience the odd mis-step and you might even go backwards. The important thing is to ensure that the "retreating is fleeting". But frothy ideas like this are not new. Proverbs (17:22) states that "a merry heart doeth good like medicine".

The idea, frothy or not, has been explored in a number of studies that have sought to examine whether any significant, causal relationship exists between the use and production of humour − or the expression of a specific humour style or collection of humour styles − and well-being and health. One of the earliest was that of Rod Martin and Herbert Lefcourt (1983), who found that negative events and mood disturbances were less strongly correlated in people scoring high on humour. Later studies were mixed: one found no evidence that humour moderated people's responses to stress or physical

DOI: 10.4324/9780429347269-5

illness (Porterfield, 1987), while another found that humour moderated people's responses to depression but not anxiety (Nezu, Nezu & Blissett, 1988). Some studies have directly examined the effect of exposure to comedy on self-reports of well-being, mood and pain. The majority, however, have undertaken correlational studies of participants who self-report their degree of health, life satisfaction, sense of humour and personality.

The Humor Styles Questionnaire (HSQ) has been used to study correlationally a wide range of positive and negative behaviour, as you saw in the section on personality. Positive humour styles have been associated with increased social competence, happiness, perceived social support, life satisfaction and resilience (Fitts, Sebby & Zlokovich, 2009; Ford et al., 2016; Ford, McCreight & Richardson, 2014; Dyck & Holtzman, 2013; Cann & Collette, 2014). They have been associated with lower loneliness, shyness, depression, neuroticism, social anxiety and suicidal ideation (Fitts et al., 2009; Tucker et al., 2013; Dyck & Holtzman, 2013). Self-enhancing humour has been correlated with self-reports of more positive emotions and fewer chronic worries (Cann & Cann, 2013; Cann & Collette, 2014).

Cann and Collette measured the relationship between emotional stability, humour styles and well-being over two months in a group of 120 introductory psychology students. Being emotionally stable predicted resilience and psychological well-being; self-enhancing humour positively correlated with positive emotion and negatively correlated with low emotional stability.

Rumination and depressive symptoms also may benefit from affiliative or self-enhancing humour (Olson, Hugelshofer, Kwon & Reff, 2005). Olson et al. found that high levels of both acted as a buffer against the type of rumination associated with depressive thoughts, suggesting that individuals who expressed these high levels shift their rumination towards an amusing part of their distress to cheer themselves up. However, people scoring high on the HSQ have also been found to take a less serious approach to their life, which may lead to unhealthy habits such as substance use (Edwards & Martin, 2012).

Negative humour styles have been associated with decreased happiness and increased suicidal ideation, physical symptoms of ill health, neuroticism and depression (Dyck & Holtzman, 2013; Fitts et al., 2009; Ford et al., 2014, 2016; Tucker et al., 2013). The research, therefore, suggests that two of the HSQ styles are associated with positive behaviour, particularly emotional behaviour, and the other two are associated with poorer emotional/psychological well-being.

A meta-analysis of 37 studies examining the relationship between HSQ scores and mental health confirmed this pattern in general, except for one specific finding. It found a positive relationship between the positive styles and positive well-being/mental health, but it also found that self-defeating humour was associated with poorer mental health and that the aggressive style showed little relationship with mental health (Schneider, Voracek & Tran, 2018).

Two diary studies have examined the relationship between humour styles and work and romantic relationship satisfaction (Guenter, Schreurs, Van Emmerik, Gijsbers & Van Iterson, 2013; Caird & Martin, 2014). Guenter et al. asked 57 Dutch employees to keep a diary for two weeks and found a correlation between the use of adaptive humour and greater engagement in work and between the use of mal-adaptive humour and greater emotional exhaustion. Others' reactions to the humour did not affect these relationships. Caird and Martin asked 136 undergraduates to keep a diary over three weeks, specifically asking them to note their relationship satisfaction with their romantic partners and the humour styles they used. Affiliative styles were positively associated with relationship satisfaction; self-defeating humour was negatively correlated with relationship satisfaction but only in those individuals who typically use high levels of this style of humour.

A later study used the HSQ and other measures in a diary study of 123 German and Swiss young (average age, 24 years) adults (Heintz, 2017). This study wanted to examine humour behaviours, rather than styles. Heintz's analysis utilised seven of these humour behaviours or dimensions: cheerful, witty, deriding, amused, sarcastic, self-directed and canned (jokes, nonsense rhymes rather than the conventional meaning of artificially added laughter). She found correlations between these behaviours and personality measures. The emphasis on behaviours is important because one criticism of the HSQ has been its validity. For example, Ruch and Heintz (2017) have argued that its items conflate content with context and that when context is removed from the items (social settings, intentions, mood), the correlations between the styles and well-being disappear.

If there is a relationship between humour use/style and well-being (and the evidence overwhelmingly suggests that there is), then why? What might underpin this relationship? What does humour do to create this effect? One explanation might be cognitive reappraisal: the ability to interpret negative events positively, and that this is what humour enables (Fritz, 2020). By viewing negative events less negatively (or more positively), we better manage possible stress. Humour – or our use of it – makes us resilient, in other words. Fritz cites a substantial body of evidence showing that the use of humour is associated with more positive appraisal of negative events occurring in controlled laboratory settings and in real life (e.g., Fritz, Russek & Dillon, 2017).

To answer the question of why such appraisal has this effect, Fritz argues that it may lead to a person placing events in a wider context and minimising the short-term negative impact, or they may take away a positive message from a negative event, thus giving them some degree of control over how they feel. In relation to the first proposal, people who were asked how they felt about the 9/11 attacks in the United States, for example, were found to demonstrate greater cognitive appraisal if they were dispositionally humorous and that this appraisal was associated with experiencing less distress one to three months after the attack. Self-enhancing humour was the most significant influence. Two studies reported that cognitive reappraisal mediated the use of this humour style: it reduced psychological distress in undergraduates who were coping with stressors and with the events of 9/11. Self-enhancing humour style is also associated with greater persistence on a tough laboratory task (Fritz et al., 2017; Cheng & Wang, 2015).

Two other studies Fritz cites appear to support her view: one showing that self-enhancing humour is associated with finding a positive message in a traumatic life event (Boerner, Joseph & Murphy, 2017) and another showing that a style similar to self-enhancing humour is associated with reduced cardiovascular mortality and reduced mortality resulting from infection (Romundstad, Svebak, Holen & Holmen, 2016), although the usual caveats apply regarding cause and effect. The opposite style – the self-defeating style, which is characterised by a self-critical and self-handicapping way of behaving – has been associated with negative cognitive appraisal of negative events. She concedes that expending effort on continually cognitively re-appraising a negative event with no positive resolution may be maladaptive.

A second mechanism, perceived social support, may be important because people scoring high in self-enhancing and affiliative humour have greater social support and supportive relationships, whereas people high in self-defeating humour show the opposite. Aggressive humour does not appear to be meaningfully associated with perceived social support (see later). Fritz et al. (2017) found that perceived social support mediated the relationship between humour style and psychological distress, with those high in affiliative and self-enhancing humour receiving the greatest social support; those high in self-defeating humour were less likely to receive social support and therefore experienced greater distress.

The lack of a meaningful relationship between an aggressive humour style and social support is interesting because this relationship seems a lot more complex than the others. For example, Fritz et al. (2017) found that high levels of aggressive humour successfully moderated high degrees of stress so that these individuals experienced less psychological distress and received some protection from their aggressive cascara compared to low-aggressive individuals. Aggressive humour is regarded as maladaptive because its aim is to demean or denigrate one individual at the expense of another, and it has been associated with spitefulness, anger, social undesirability and cyberbullying (Sari, 2016).

But this may be too simplistic a view. In fact, it is a too simplistic a view because the target audience of the humour may be an influential variable. That is, a socially competent user of aggressive humour will be adept at determining when to use aggressive humour and will tailor this to his or her audience. Some studies suggest that the affiliative and self-enhancing types are also the most interpersonally adept but those who are self-defeating types are the least adept (Falanga, De Caroli & Sagone, 2014; Salavera, Usán & Jarie, 2020; Yip & Martin, 2006).

Those less adept at taking the social temperature in the room will be destined to be banished to the social Antarctica of human relations. Fritz's (2020) study of 108 undergraduates found that self-enhancing and affiliative humour styles were associated with less psychological distress and better physical health, but this relationship was mediated by greater reappraisal and social support. People scoring high on aggressive humour and those with the least competent interpersonal relations received less positive social support and experienced greater distress, a finding that was replicated in a 10-week study of 193 undergraduates. This study also found that the use of self-defeating humour was associated with more health difficulties over time and that affiliative and self-enhancing humour was associated with fewer health difficulties. Aggressive humour users experienced more health difficulties across time, although this relationship was mediated by receiving less social support and experiencing fewer positive social media interactions.

THE DARK SIDE OF HUMOUR

A dominant theory of humour and laugher, as you saw in Chapter 2, argues that one use of humour is to disparage others, alienate outgroups and increase the power and strength of the person using humour at the expense of the humour's target. Examples include the schadenfreude a person experiences at the comical come-uppance of an unpleasant individual (a public put-down or a messy accident), the mirth generated by a person slipping on ice or off a roof a la *You've*

Been Framed, a prospective president being roasted at a public event for his vanity and narcissism, a group of actors being excoriated at an awards ceremony ("I like a drink as much as the next man, so long as the next man isn't Mel Gibson"), the satirising of a (fictional) bomb-mad US general and the quotidian undermining of a colleague or friend with whom we disagree. Disparagement humour is a common method of demonstrating control or giving us control over a person or an event that would not be possible directly. It is common expression of feeling that can be cathartic and positive at one end of the continuum. At the other, it can be demonstrably brutal, aggressive and hurtful, and, as we saw in the section on humour styles, people who score highly on the Aggressive Humour style of the HSQ are not those who are perceived as the most likeable or who have the most positive interpersonal relations. No one likes living permanently with Chandler from *Friends*.

In humour research, there has been an obvious focus on aggressive and self-defeating humour styles because these are part of a widely used measure. However, other studies have examined the relationship between humour, humour styles and other darker aspects of human personality. Some of the more obvious melanic traits in psychology are the Dark Tetrad, a set of personality traits representing Narcissism, Psychopathy, Machiavellianism and Sadism. Other studies have examined trait spitefulness, anger, prejudice and borderline personality. The Dark Tetrad began life as the Dark Triad, a term used by Paulhus and Williams (2002) to describe the first three of the traits in the Dark Tetrad; the fourth was added later. These traits have been defined as "the pursuit of gratification from vanity or egotistic admiration of one's attributes" (narcissism); "a duplicitous interpersonal style, a cynical disregard for morality, and a focus on self-interest and personal gain" (Machiavellianism); and "a personality trait characterised by enduring antisocial behaviour, diminished empathy and remorse, and disinhibited or bold behaviour" (psychopathy) (Muris, Merckelbach, Otgaar & Meijer, 2017). Sadism describes an enjoyment in the deliberate infliction of harm and injury to others or seeing others being harmed or injured.

Machiavellianism, named after Niccolo Machiavelli, the author of *The Prince* (1532), describes a cynical, manipulative and exploitative person who uses nefarious means to achieve personal outcomes. Typical quotes from Machiavelli's book include: "If an injury has to be done to a man it should be so severe that his vengeance need not be feared" and "it is much safer to be feared than loved". Narcissism, named after the comely young Greek hunter who fell in love with his own reflection, describes a personality who is grandiosely obsessed with his or her own importance to the exclusion of actual evidence, a person who has an exaggerated view of his or her own abilities, is exhibitionistic and envious and enjoys experiencing a sense of superiority over others, believing that they are superior to others; their positive outlook tends to be undermined if they perceive a threat to their self through criticism or the absence of adulation.

Psychopathy has a deep history in psychology and criminology (and ancient history – the original psychopath was described by Theophrastus) and has gone through various nomenclaturic iterations over centuries (from sociopath, to anti-social personality disorder [ASPD], to psychopath). The current conception is derived from Cleckley's list of personality traits, which he described in his book, *Mask of Sanity*. It is often conflated and confused with ASPD, but the creator of the tool which determines the diagnosis of psychopathy argues that it is distinct and different from ASPD because the latter lacks the manipulative and emotional features of psychopathy and instead is characterised by anti-social behaviour and violence/criminality. Psychopaths express both, but are also charming, supremely manipulative and utterly ruthless. Measures of psychopathy tend to comprise four sub-components: psychopaths score highly on all; ASPD score highly on two. Psychopathy is associated with lack of care/empathy for others, manipulativeness, violence, criminality and callousness.

People who score highly on the Dark Triad tend to score highly on all sorts of maladaptive and malevolent behaviour, including financial misconduct, sexual deviance, cyberbullying, cheating, racism and schadenfreude (Muris et al., 2017), and the three traits are significantly inter-related and correlated. However, the dominant trait seems to be psychopathy – this is the trait that most accurately and consistently predicts other transgressive behaviours.

The first study of the Dark Triad and humour styles was published in 2010 by Veselka et al. It found that people scoring on psychopathy and Machiavellianism also scored high for aggressive humour and self-defeating humour, whereas people scoring high for narcissism showed little affiliative humour. An extension of Veselka et al.'s study, published in 2012, found that Machiavellianism and psychopathy were positively correlated with aggressive humour and self-defeating humour in 200 university undergraduates and showed no relationship with the other two styles. Narcissism, as in the earlier study, was correlated with affiliative humour but also with aggressive humour. A study of extreme personality traits in 574 same-sex adult dizygotic and monozygotic twins (borderline personality disorder [BPD], characterised by engagement in self harm, including suicide, and which is correlated with anxiety, depression, hostility and impulsiveness) found that affiliative and self-enhancing humour types were negatively correlated with BPD and positively correlated with aggressive and self-defeating styles (Schermer et al., 2015). Similar results were found in a later study, which reported that negative emotion and detachment were negatively correlated with affiliative and self-enhancing humour in 594 college students (Zeigler-Hill, McCabe & Vrabel, 2016). Being antagonistic was associated with having an aggressive humour style and negatively correlated with having an affiliative humour style. Being disinhibited was associated with aggressive humour, and this and psychoticism were related to the self-defeating humour style.

Those who see themselves as socially dominant but also show anti-black prejudice have been found to use aggressive humour more; having a right-wing, authoritarian disposition has not been found to be significantly related to any humour style (Hodson, Macinnis & Rush, 2010). A specific type of aggressive humour (sarcasm) has been found to be associated with the trait anger – being a very angry person predicts self-reported use of sarcasm (Szymaniak & Kalowski, 2020).

Spiteful people are also more likely to exhibit negative humour styles. Spiteful people are "willing to incur a cost in order to inflict harm on another individual" and have been found to show low levels of guilt and empathy. A study of 593 undergraduate students found that self-reported spitefulness was positively correlated with aggressive and self-defeating humour and negatively correlated with affiliative and self-enhancing humour (Vrabel, Ziegler-Hill & Shango, 2017).

CREATING OFFENCE I

As the last section demonstrated, for an art form and an act of creation that is designed to bring joy and pleasure, comedy does have its dark side. Comedy can be dangerous. And some people, some organisations, some countries flinch from comic inspection and ridicule. Satire – ridiculing the vice and folly of the times – is one type of humour specifically used to achieve the purpose of annoying and undermining those in power, the idiotic and the harmful by exposing them to ridicule. From Juvenal and Swift's *Modest Proposal*; through to *Dr Strangelove*, 1984, *That Was the Week That Was*, *Spitting Image* and *The Daily Show*; through to *Private Eye* and *The Onion*, satire has been used to change the way we think, with variable success. It is a cliche-but a cliche is a cliche because it's true-to say that the relentless hammering Margaret Thatcher received in *Spitting Image* had a net effect of zero on her political progress and success. For example, this sketch is now legendary: Thatcher is dining with her Cabinet. The waitress asks: What will you have, sir? Thatcher replies: Steak, rare. The waitress follows up with: And the vegetables? Thatcher: Oh, they'll have the same). She, and John Major, won two election majorities during the show's run. And John Major was portrayed entirely in grey and followed a diet consisting entirely and exclusively of peas. Peter Cook famously, and sarcastically, dedicated his The Establishment Club in Soho London to the political reviews of Berlin in the 30s "which did so much to prevent the rise of Adolf Hitler".

History, even recent history, throws up examples of comic creations that have caused trouble, roused ire or provoked displeasure to such an extent that the reactions have led to sometimes fatal consequences. The offices of the mildly satirical French magazine, *Charlie*

Hebdo, were attacked on 7 January 2015 and 12 of its staff and writers murdered by Islamic terrorists after it had published a cartoon depicting the prophet Mohammad. Few news organisations and publications published the offending image for fear of death. There have been more minor but just as significant examples where taking offence at humour has led to potentially reactionary outcomes. In 2006, Rowan Atkinson campaigned against the criminalisation of criticism of religion/incitement of religious hatred when this was proposed in the UK's Serious Organised Crime and Police Bill (www.theguardian. com/politics/2006/jan/30/immigrationpolicy.religion)

In 2001, the scabrous Channel 4 comedy, *Brass Eye* fronted by Chris Morris, broadcast the subliminal message "Grade is a cunt" in its final edition, a reference to the channel controller and a response by the programme team to Grade's requests to insist on cuts to the programme. In 1997, the programme famously duped a caravan of celebrities into believing that a made-up, 12-inch, yellow, 1990s rave drug, "Cake", existed. One of the people duped and asked to participate in a public campaign against the drug was the Conservative MP for Basildon David Amess (now Sir), who even raised the scourge in Parliament. The comedian Bernard Manning described how one girl who had taken the drug had thrown up her own pelvis. The drug was repeatedly described as a "made-up drug" throughout the show.

Brass Eye also created a huge controversy with its special episode on paedophilia broadcast in 2001 ("Paedogeddon"), which was designed to lampoon the media's lurid obsession with sex offences and its fomenting of anger and agitation and subsequent public panic. The TV and radio personality, Neil Fox, was filmed informing viewers: "paedophiles have more genes in common with crabs than they do with you and me. Now that is scientific fact – there's no real evidence for it – but it is scientific fact". Until the BBC's blanket coverage of the death of the Duke of Edinburgh in 2020, it was the most complained about British TV show. More recently, the former estate agent and Vine sensation, Dapper Laughs, was removed from his ITV television series following the response to comments he was recorded making about rape at his live stage show. His mea culpa interview with the *Newsnight* journalist, Emily Maitlis, is worth watching (www.youtube.com/watch?v=lBt3fr5viAE).

Maitlis also interviewed the BBC director general following the live broadcast of a boorish exchange on radio between Jonathan Ross and Russell Brand. They left a message on the actor Andrew Sachs's answerphone saying that Brand had had sex with Sachs's grand-daughter. Both were later suspended from their presenting jobs. During the interview, Maitlis raised other examples with the director general which had troubled the BBC Trust, including Frankie Boyle's now notorious joke on the BBC2 show, *Mock the Week*. Improvising a response to the challenge "things you wouldn't hear the Queen say during her Christmas broadcast" on the show, Boyle responded: "I'm now so old that my pussy is haunted". Its notoriety coincided with the Ross/Brand controversy. The joke itself, however, had been broadcast on at least two occasions previously and had received six complaints.

Some jokes, for reasons of "taste", never get past the starting block. Alan Zweibel's warm, informative and funny book about his life as a comedy writer on *Saturday Night Live*, *Curb Your Enthusiasm* and with Garry Shandling describes one joke for a sketch that never made it onto *SNL*. The idea was to come up with the worst Hannukah presents. The rejected idea was a set of drums for Ann Frank. You can see why it never got on air.

David Steel, the leader of the Liberal Party in the UK from 1976 to 1988 and then joint leader of the SDP-Liberal Alliance with his more suave, urbane and dashing partner Dr David Owen, bemoaned his depiction in the rubbery puppet satire series, *Spitting Image*, as a redundant, irrelevant, hamster-like accessory to Owen (who was depicted in the show carrying around Steel in his suit breast pocket). Steel, who was no hamster at only a couple of inches shorter than Owen, conceded that this representation of him as Lilliputian, docile and pliant probably harmed his public perception as joint leader and magnified the status of his partner. Some, of course, liked their depiction in *Spitting Image* – Michael Heseltine, Deputy PM from 1995 to 1997, by all accounts, asked the makers if he could buy his puppet. He was regularly portrayed as a wildly coiffed, gung-ho, camouflage-clad, face-painted warrior.

In June 2020, following the Black Lives Matter protests, a number of famous comedy shows were removed from some online platforms and streaming services because of the depiction of white comedians "blacking up", among them *Come Fly With Me*, *Little Britain* and *Bo Selecta*. One episode of *Fawlty Towers* was temporarily removed from the cable station UKTV, a station owned by BBC Studios, because of its use of offensive racial language by one of its dozy, reactionary characters (the Major).

Sometimes characters are created to express vile views with the intention of highlighting those views and ridiculing them. A good example is Alf Garnett, a character created by Johnny Speight in his sitcom *Till Death Us Do Part* (first broadcast in 1965), who is depicted as a bigot who expresses vinegary views about all sorts of people – black people, young people and politicians, especially. Intended to be a character to be laughed at, some viewers were more sympathetic to Garnett than Sleight had anticipated. The show was translated to the United States in *All in the Family* (later, *Archie Bunker's Place*) and featured a blue-collar bigot called Archie Bunker played by Carroll O'Connor. It was a successful couple of shows running from 1971 to 1983.

A similar unintended fate befell Harry Enfield's Loadsamoney character from *Saturday Live* in 1986 in which a gobby, Thatcher-era, faded-jeans-sporting plasterer (played by Enfield) boasts about how much money he is making. He regularly flaunted piles of cash in his fists, shaking them at the camera, taunting his poorer – probably Labour-supporting – viewers. Intended as a satire on 1980s money-grabbing gormlessness and self-interest, the character took on a life of its own and was adopted by the public as just another funny character devoid of any political meaning. He was too personable. He even had a hit record in 1988.

Some of the darker and controversial aspects of comedy are reviewed in a couple of excellent texts: Bucaria and Barra's (2016) *Taboo Comedy* published by Palgrave and Oppliger and Shouse's (2020) *The Dark Side of Stand-Up Comedy*, also published by Palgrave.

CREATING OFFENCE II: THE PSYCHOLOGY OF SWEARING (HUMOUR AS A RISKY ACTIVITY)

While some offensive comedy is culturally sanctioned (see the last section), other types aren't. The wrong joke or quip at the wrong time to the wrong person can lead not just to a social faux pas but a sacking or a punch. Humour can be risky so its manipulators need to know how to wield it and when to wield it and with whom. If it is wielded politically and sagely, none of these might happen. The application and execution of aggressive humour, for example, can be used to recruit or to consolidate group motivation or to defuse or eliminate a threat. There is some association between using aggressive humour and risky behaviour. Cann and Cann (2013) found that people who were likely to use aggressive humour perceived less risk but engaged in greater amounts of risky behaviour (e.g., unprotected sex, phoning whilst driving and so on). Allied to risky behaviour engagement is sensation-seeking, a trait identified by Zuckerman as characteristic of individuals who seek out stimulating novel experiences.

One of the riskiest behaviours in the context of humour and comedy is swearing. Imprecation has to be done delicately and deftly or it can be wildly misconstrued and considered offensive. There are still some countries with laws that prohibit it, and fines can be imposed for doing it. Hughes (1998) in his book on swearing notes that almost all societies have taboos in some form (formal or informal) against swearing. Van Lancker and Cummings define it as the "use of deistic, visceral and other taboo words and phrases" (p. 83), where deistic refers to religion-related cursing and visceral refers to body function–related cursing. Swearing is, of course, also referred to as "cursing". The use of sex-based swearing (fuck, cunt, prick, mother-fucker and so on) is virtually universal. Gallahorn (1971) categorised swearing into three categories: curse words, anal-erythral and genital, and these categories sum up the catalogue of uninhibited swearing, but it has not been the only taxonomy (others have devised 14 categories of swearing). Men, in general, tend to swear more and use a greater variety of expletives than do women (de Klerk, 1991; Foote & Woodward, 1973). Various surveys of swearing have found that the most commonly used swear words are "fuck", "cunt", "shit", "hell", "God", "damn" and "bitch". Fewer of the stronger (genital) ones appear in samples of older participants.

Jay (1980, 2009) identified 18 swear words commonly used by a sample of over-45s with "hell", "godamn", "shit" and "Jesus" accounting for 57% of them. Some neurological conditions feature symptoms that include automatic and involuntary swearing. The most well-known of these is the movement disorder, Gilles de la Tourette, principally characterised by involuntary tics (the disorder is thought to be attributable to a dysfunctional basal ganglia/frontal lobe and the connections between them) but 20% to 50% of patients also exhibit coprolalia (swearing), and there are differences between speakers from different nations in terms of the swearing they generate, although "fuck", "shit", "whore" and "shut up" are common in virtually all (Van Lancker & Cummings, 1999).

Comedy is a ruthless exploiter of swearing. A survey of 821 participants who rated 5000 English words for funniness found that the word "fuck" was one of the funniest words in the list – it appeared in the top 1% (Engelthaler & Hills, 2018). Finding good examples of the use of swearing in comedy is not difficult. The plosives and fricatives common to the most widely used swear words lend themselves to prosody and vocal delivery, punctuating metre with a cadence that adds power and glee to an otherwise prosaic line (swearing has been associated with increased heart rate and galvanic skin response and greater tolerance of pain; Stephens & Robertson, 2020). Lenny Bruce's 1965 autobiography was titled "*How to Talk Dirty and Influence People*". Chaucer was a devil at it (see The Miller's Tale), and written text commonly features it. Billy Connolly, a maestro of the well-timed imprecation, made the case for the defence in *Tall Tales and Wee Stories*:

> I don't understand the snobbishness about swearing. I grew up swearing. Everybody around me swore. It's part of our culture. It can be poetic. It can be violent, and it can be very funny. It's the

rhythm of how we speak, and the colour of how we communi-
cate. So, if you're likely to be offended by the swearing, you may
as well fuck off now.

(p. 7)

Mass visual forms were slow to match the liberal flow of the written word. The first recorded use of the word "fuck" (although this has
been challenged) on television occurred in 1965 in the UK by the
theatre critic and National Theatre's literary manager, Kenneth Tynan.
There's even a 2005 documentary, *Fuck*, which chronicles the word's
history and use. Films which are prolific expressers of the word are
not comedies, but grittier adult dramas or thrillers. *Twin Town*, the
1997 Swansea-based comedy, is probably the filthiest comedy, with
318 uses of the word (*Jay and Silent Bob Strike Back* featured 248). Richard
Curtis's first lines of dialogue in *Four Weddings and a Funeral* are the word
"fuck" said four times, followed by "fuckety fuck", then "bugger",
and this is a charming, if unexpected, beginning to what is, to all
intents a purposes, a romantic comedy. One of *Die Hard*'s most famous
lines, Yipee-kay-ay, mother-fucker" is routinely replaced by censori-
ous TV controllers with "Yipee-kay-ay, Mister Falcon/Melon Farmer",
which is as baffling as it is nonsensical. Nick Frost and Simon Pegg
even went so far as to create a sanitised version of their second Cor-
netto instalment, *Hot Fuzz*, and put it on the DVD as an extra (calling
it Hot Funk). One of the most famous scenes in Larry David's *Curb
Your Enthusiasm* concerns a family's reaction to a typographical error in
the newspaper obituary of a beloved aunt, in which "beloved aunt"
becomes "beloved cunt".

Armando Iannucci's television comedy series about the digestive
system of government and Opposition, *The Thick of It*, a show never shy
of releasing the occasional "cunt" or "fuck", holds the record for the
most "fucks" uttered in a TV series (one every 12 seconds in episode
7 of season 3). It is an excellent example of the deft use of swearing
for comic effect. Its swearing is almost incontinent. The series is set
inside a fictional government department but reflects the interactions
of, and insecurities between, politicians, their special advisors and

journalists. It is held together by the sweary glue that is Malcolm Tucker (Peter Capaldi), the government's chief spin doctor (director of communications). Tucker prowls his Whitehall departments like a relentlessly angry ocelot on the verge of an aneurysm, desperately seeking prey to shit on in the most spectacularly diarrheic fashion. His most endearing response to a knock on the door is: "Come the fuck in, or fuck the fuck off". A typical Tucker exchange is this, which occurs in the control suite of a BBC radio station where a minister of state, Nicola Murray, is on air as a critical comment from Tim in Ruislip comes through to the editor who is planning on forwarding it to the host:

Malcolm: That's your fucking career over, right, OK, you're fucking dead. And those three little words, "Tim in Ruislip", are the fucking nails in your coffin, dear. (mimes hammering nails into wood) Tim. In. Ruislip. Tim in fucking Ruislip. And as for Tim in fucking –

Janice: Yeah, okay, can you stop fucking saying that, please?

Malcolm: – FUCKING, fucking Ruislip, he's fucking dead as well! That fucking texting coward. Give me his number. What's his fucking number? Give me the fucking number of Tim in Ruislip.

Janice (to a colleague): Erase it. Take it off the screen now.

Malcolm: If you don't give me his fucking number, do you know what I'm gonna have to do? I'm gonna have to fucking go to fucking Ruislip, and fucking snap the thumb and forefinger off of every single person I see, who I think resembles the kind of wanker that would be walking around in this day and fucking age with a name like fucking Tim! How do you think that sounds, huh?

Stewart Pearson (Tucker's opposite number): Quite, quite mad.

The later defenestration of Pearson (Vincent Franklin), leads to the following lament by the character:

You know, I've spent ten years detoxifying this party. It's been a bit like renovating an old, old house, yeah? You can take out a

> sexist beam here, a callous window there, replace the odd homo-
> phobic roof tile. But after a while you realise that this renovation
> is doomed. Because the foundations are built on what I can only
> describe as a solid bed of cunts. Drew et al (2009)

So, the deft application of the occasional, pungent, forceful swear
word can make highly crafted, crystallised comedy. This is the world
of fiction and entertainment, but in everyday life, the same applies.
Kennison and Messer (2017) suggested that swearing was considered
a form of social risk taking, which it is. You rarely hear swearing being
used in the demotic in parliaments or in senates and hardly ever in
religious contexts or even in formal work contexts unless the context specifically requires it. Kennison and Messer found that swearers
tended to be sensation-seekers and risk-takers, engaging in behaviour such as substance use. In their 2018 study of 333 undergraduates, they found that sensation-seeking scores (specifically, thrill and
adventure seeking) predicted affiliative and aggressive humour styles
in men and aggressive and self-defeating styles in women. Swearing
predicted aggressive humour styles in both sexes, affiliative humour
for men and self-defeating humour use in women. As is typical in
these studies, men were more likely to use higher levels of aggressive
humour, showed greater sensation-seeking and swore more than did
women. A related study which examined the relationship between
humour styles, trait cheerfulness, playfulness and substance use found
a positive correlation between affiliative humour, aggressive humour
and substance use, but this relationship was mediated by seriousness
(Edwards & Martin, 2012). That is, people high in humour and who
are more playful/less serious were those most likely to use alcohol,
cigarettes, marijuana and cocaine.

People are also more likely to be risk averse when making decisions about life dilemmas and investment decisions when they have
been exposed to happy film clips (Lin et al., 2006). There are even
competing models that predict the outcome of being in a good
mood – the affect infusion model argues that being in a positive
mood makes us more risk prone, whereas the mood-maintenance

hypothesis argues that being in a good mood makes us more cautious. Both were tested in an unusual way by Gabriele Lepori at Keele University (Lepori, 2015). She examined the relationship between US stock market performance and the theatrical release of comedy movies in North America using data from 1994 to 2010. She found that an increase in the release of comedy films at a weekend was correlated with a decrease in stock returns on the following Monday which, at a stretch, supports the mood-maintenance model because positive mood led to decreased risk-taking with the knock-on effects on the stock market. Of course, this study is correlational with all the caveats that are usually hung on such studies.

HUMOUR IN PSYCHOTHERAPY

Everyone knows the hoary cliche about laughter being the best medicine – and the evidence for this is reviewed later – but there are some cases, therapeutic cases, where you might not expect humour to be appropriate or to work. One such case is psychotherapy – a view that's succinctly summarised by Kubie (1970): "Humor has its place in life. Let us keep it there by acknowledging that one place where it has very limited role, if any, is in psychotherapy" (p. 866). But as Rod Martin (2017) notes in his chapter on the uses of humour in psychotherapy, there has been a small industry of research on how humour can be used to (1) effect a good outcome in psychotherapy, (2) improve interaction between client and therapist, (3) put the client at ease by establishing rapport and (4) encouraging reflection and enhancing the closeness of the client-therapist relationship. Fry and Salameh's (1987) *Handbook of Humour and Psychotherapy* contains around 300 books, articles and other materials attesting to the importance of laughter and humour in psychotherapy.

Laughter occurs often during psychotherapy – around every three minutes according to one study (Marci, Moran & Orr, 2004) – and most of this is produced by the client (Dionigi & Canestrari, 2018). Martin notes that some early schools of psychotherapy explicitly encouraged or endorsed the use of humour in settings such as these, and this is true. One well-known therapy, Albert Ellis's rational emotive therapy, recommends that therapists challenge clients' absurd, irrational or unrealistic beliefs and thoughts and approves the use of humour, even sarcasm, to help facilitate this. It is, as Martin concludes, quite confrontational.

The number of studies on the direct effects of the uses of humour within a psychotherapeutic context is few and beset with methodological issues and problems, some of which include a failure to include an adequate control group, inconsistency in therapist (this is inevitable), inconsistent scripts and failure of participant randomisation. One well-known (in this field) example of the successful use of humour in a specific form of therapy (more correctly, a behavioural therapy – you'll see why) involved studying people with arachnophobia. Ventis, Higbee and Murdock (2001) found that the inclusion of humour into systematic desensitisation led to a reduction in fear of spiders compared to a no-treatment control group. Systematic desensitisation (SD) is a cognitive behavioural method of reducing a phobia by gradually exposing the participant (the "systematic" part) to the feared object with the aim of gradually blunting the fear response (the "desensitisation" part). The study was small (40 undergraduates) but well-designed. There were weekly sessions over four weeks, and participants received traditional SD or SD with humour or no SD. The humour component involved asking participants to create amusing statements about spiders and create funny images about spiders.

The use of humour by therapists as a part of therapy has also been the subject of a few studies and very few of these allow us to conclude anything meaningful. Some of the protocols can be quite artificial – one study asked people to view a tape of a therapy session in which humour was or was not used and asked participants (viewers) how likely they would be to want to be seen by the therapist (Rosenheim & Golan, 1986). Viewers preferred the therapist who didn't deploy humour. A different study, using a similar protocol, did find a positive effect of humour use. Viewers regarded a therapist who used humour as being more approachable and a better facilitator of a positive relationship than one who used humour derisively (Foster & Reid, 1983).

In a study where 85 therapy sessions were videotaped, humorous interventions produced no better benefits than did non-humorous interventions. It also found that around 20% of the humour interactions were derisive (Killinger, 1987). The percentage using this type of humour in another study of group therapy, and by the group not the therapist, was around 75%, with the humour directed towards other group members or people outside the group (Peterson & Pollio, 1982). The opposite pattern is seen in interactions with physicians, where humour might be better applied because it can leaven the nature and response to the illness; if a physician deploys positive attempts at humour, patients tend to come away more satisfied (Sala, Krupat & Roter, 2002); the more satisfied they were, the more likely they were to laugh during their visits.

The evidence for the efficacy of humour in psychotherapy settings, therefore, is thin and the area is beset with methodological problems.

HUMOUR AND PHYSICAL HEALTH

The links between humour, whether it is sense of humour or humour styles, and physical health – while they may seem plausible – are supported by very little empirical evidence. Dyck and Holtzman (2013), one of the few studies in this area, found that self-enhancing humour was associated with fewer self-reports of symptoms of physical ill health and self-defeating with more. Fritz (2020) found a similar result in her study of 108 undergraduates, but that affiliative humour also correlated positively with reports of fewer self-reported health difficulties (which included the number of days they had been ill, activities that had been curtailed because of ill health and so on). In a second study in which she measured health difficulties and psychological distress over 10 weeks, she found that self-defeating humour was associated with increasing health difficulties across the course of the study, a finding that was mediated by those people having less social support. Two studies therefore suggest that certain types of humour styles are associated with fewer symptoms of ill health and some with more. Note, however, that these are two studies, and like most of these studies of humour styles, the results are correlational.

Another study found that there was no association between having better health habits and humour but did find a correlation between high sense of humour and less fear of death and of serious illness and less concern about pain (Kuiper & Nicholl, 2004). A longitudinal study of 34 Finnish police chiefs, who were tested in 1995 and 1998, found no significant correlation between humour scores and physical health or psychological well-being (Kerkkanen, Kuiper & Martin, 2004). This group also looked at some additional police constables and found that the association with humour was negative – high humour scores were associated with increased smoking and greater risk of cardiovascular disease.

LAUGHTER THERAPY

One of the most famous books in the psychology of humour – so famous that any book on the psychology of humour can't help but mention it – is Norman Cousins's 1979 book, *The Anatomy of Illness*. It is famous because in it, Cousins recounts his recovery from a degenerative spinal injury via the use of laughter. Since then, a number of books and practical applications have been produced extolling the power of laughter and how it may heal psychological – and even physical – wounds and ailments. Laughter Club, for example, is one organisation that uses laughter yoga and simulated laughter in particular to lift mood and improve well-being. It involves encouraging participants in groups to laugh and have them engage in relaxation exercises. Robert Holden's *Laughter – The Best Medicine* suggests uplifting your spirits through "happy breathing, simulated smiles and transcendental breathing". Don your "Super-Humour-Person cape and save the world from the arch-villain Over-Seriousness", it exhorts. And, then, once you've put your cape on, "run without fun". Why? Because if you do not, "your stride will falter", as we saw right at the beginning of this chapter.

While the marble-losing prose might be off-putting, there is a grain of truth in these bland, cursory homilies and it is this: the expression of laughter, especially simulated laughter, has been associated with improvements or perceived improvements in psychological well-being. However, caveats apply that are the size of icebergs, and we will examine these shortly. The effect of laughter on physical health – that is, the significant and positive alteration of physical ill health as a result of the production of laughter – is much less clear-cut. We will take a look at this evidence shortly, too. As van der Wal and Kok wrote in 2019, "scientific research is still in an early stage when it comes to empirically determining the therapeutic value of laughter" (p. 473). So, what do we know?

Two reviews have recently examined the effectiveness of laughter therapy on psychological and physical health. Mora-Ripoll from the Laughter Research Network in Spain identified five types of laughter employed in these studies (Mora-Ripoll, 2011). The first is genuine or spontaneous laughter, which is our natural, uninhibited, involuntary reaction to external stimulation. The second is "simulated laughter" which is self-stimulated, not provoked by any external stimulus, and has no purpose in terms of achieving joy or pleasure. This type appears to be particularly important. "Stimulated laughter" is that which is provoked by direct external stimulation (e.g., being tickled, having your knee squeezed). "Induced laughter" describes the laughter provoked by medication or alcohol. Finally, "pathological laughter" is produced as a result of neural dysfunction or brain injury.

Mora-Ripoll examined studies from oncology, dermatology, immunology, cardiology, psychiatry and a host of other disciplines. The review found positive associations between laughter and muscle relaxation, improved respiration, stress hormone reduction, immune system function increase and pain tolerance. The psychological effects, however, were much stronger than any physical ones, and the review found that humour was used as a coping mechanism more than it was used for any other purpose. Laughter was associated with a reduction in stress, anxiety and tension; an elevation in mood, self-esteem, hope and energy; memory and creativity enhancement; improvement in interpersonal interaction and attraction to others; increased friendliness and helpfulness; improvements in psychological well-being and quality of life; and increased contagiousness (laughter begat laughter). Nine of the studies included used simulated laughter as a stimulus. A naturalistic diary study (Vlahovic et al., 2012) of 41 participants who were asked to keep a record of when and how they laughed and in what context found that happiness was only related to the duration of laughter in interactions in physical face-to-face contexts (not email, Skype, messaging and other non-contact media).

One study of 53 undergraduates examined the effect of listening to comedy on people's anticipation of threat – electrodes were attached to them, which they were told would deliver a shock at the end of 12 minutes (this was the late 1980s, strangely, when you might have thought such procedures had been banned). The study found that listening to US stand-up comedians was associated with experiencing less stress and anxiety than was listening to a geology lesson or no stimulus (Yovetich, Dale & Hudak, 1990).

A more recent review by researchers at the Universities of Leeds and Vrije (van der Wal & Kok, 2019) makes the common observation that this type of humour study is methodologically very problematic. There is no control group, there are small group sizes (on average, 68 participants; 12 studies had fewer than 20 participants), randomisation is almost non-existent, there are a myriad of confounds and results are often correlational – there are very few empirical studies. The long-term benefits, such as they are, were also not examined, as there is very rarely a follow-up. The English/Dutch study identified 29 studies they included in a meta-analysis and 86 they included in a qualitative analysis. Depression, anxiety and stress were the most common dependent variables in the quantitative studies. Overall, they found that the association between simulated laughter production and positive effects on depression and anxiety was stronger than the association between spontaneous laughter and these outcomes. Effect sizes were twice as large. Less stress was associated with increased laughter, but laughter had no effect on the secretion of cortisol. However, there was evidence of significant publication bias – i.e., there was the publication of positive results to a degree that was not credible. The small group sizes referred to earlier were also problematic, leading van der Wal and Kok to regard these more as pilot studies than major studies.

These two syntheses suggest two things: Yes, laughter is associated with positive outcomes, but this is qualified by the understanding that the body of research in general is very poor and monumentally susceptible to publication bias. Run without fun, and you will basically still carry on running regardless.

COMEDY AND PAIN

In Sri Lanka, according to one account, laughter has quite a spectacular role (Rhodes, 1983). It is thought to purify the blood and the body and to exorcise the individual of pain-causing demons. It is literally thought to alleviate pain, although the mechanism is a little mystical and would not withstand scientific scrutiny. We saw earlier how Cousins had recounted his self-reported recovery from painful illness via judicious expressions of analgesic laughter. Whether laughter can mitigate the effects of actual pain – as opposed to stress or psychological ill health – has been the subject of a small but influential pool of studies, some of which have serious limitations. One, which won't be reported here, aimed to study the relationship between exposure to comedy and pain ratings but failed to include statistical analysis because the participants were unable to complete the pain scale used. Another study which used the cold-pressor test – a method of experimentally inducing (harmless) pain by asking participants to place their non-dominant forearm in a receptacle of ice-cold water – found that exposure to a comedy film did not make the pain any less tolerable than did a documentary film, but an examination of the ratings of the comedy used shows that, on average, it was not perceived as particularly funny, scoring 3.7 on a 7-point scale. These are the sorts of elementary scientific mistakes that were not unusual in humour/comedy studies in the 1980s and before but were published.

Probably the earliest study to show that comedy did alleviate physical suffering was Cogan, Cogan, Waltz, and McCue's (1987) study, which found that 20 men and women's discomfort thresholds were higher after having listened to a 20-minute laughter cassette than a relaxation tape or a dull narrative. Again, note the small sample sizes and that this study examined the effect of laughter (specifically), not the effect of listening to the cause of laughter (the comedy).

In an extension and development of studies such as these, Zweyer, Velker and Ruch (2004) allocated 56 women to three groups in which they watched a funny film while either getting into a cheerful mood without smiling or laughing, while smiling and laughing a lot or while commentating comedically on the film they were watching. The cold-pressor test was used to induce pain before, immediately after and 20 minutes after watching the film. Pain tolerance and thresholds increased from before to after in all three conditions, especially when individuals were expressively demonstrating their enjoyment. The group also looked at personality traits, finding that individuals who were low in trait seriousness had higher tolerance of pain. The authors acknowledge the limitation of their small sample size.

Pain was measured in a different way by Dunbar et al. (2012) who, in a series of studies, required participants to wear a frozen wine-cooler sleeve or undergo wearing a sphygmomanometer (a blood pressure cuff which delivers pressure on the arm muscle) while watching a comedy or a neutral film. Laugher was measured at 15-second intervals (very crudely measuring if participants were laughing at that point or not). The comedy condition was associated with higher pain tolerance.

Whether comedy can help reduce pain or increase its tolerance consistently is still unclear. If it were clear, you might expect many more studies in the literature to support this position and that laughter or comedy might be recommended as part of an analgesic strategy for those who experience mild to chronic pain. The field is not at the stage of methodological sophistication where you can draw any meaningful conclusions, and there are issues here that persist across other, similar studies, those involving the perception of horror, for example, where the heterogeneity of horror film types and tropes makes drawing conclusions about the effect of "horror film" difficult

(Martin, 2019). A proper study needs a decent sample size, needs to control for the effect of laughter – is the laughter causing the change or the comedy (which then generates the laughter)? – and needs to include various types of comedy. Good studies will include a manipulation check – "did you find this film clip funny?", for example – but they also need to administer different types of comedy, as these might produce difference effects. Slapstick might produce different results to satire, and there are many cognitive reasons why it might.

HUMOUR, BLOOD PRESSURE AND IMMUNOGLOBULIN

A small amount of research has examined the physical effects of laughter, and the role of the brain in smiling, laughter and appreciating (and understanding humour) is the subject of the last chapter. In the context of well-being, there has been a focus on measures such as blood pressure and immunoglobulin production. Some of the early studies are beset by the same problems we described earlier: poor controls, low numbers of participants. Typical is a study of 15 men who listened to stand-up comedy and a Laurel and Hardy film and who showed higher systolic and diastolic blood pressure during the two-thirds of the examples of chuckling and laughing they produced (Fry & Savin, 1988). The length of laughter correlated with increases in blood pressure (increases that are also seen after intense exercise). Averill's (1969) was probably the first study to examine the relationship between comedy and blood pressure, finding that this was highest when people watched sad films. However, heart rate was highest after watching a funny film.

Another study, better controlled and with a larger sample of men and women ($N = 109$), examined the relationship between coping via humour and blood pressure (Lefcourt, Davidson, Prkachin & Mills, 1997). The inclusion of both sexes was important because the study found that men and women did behave differently. Women who were higher in humour coping showed lower systolic blood pressure than low-scoring women; the opposite pattern was seen in the men, which the researchers argue is due to the high-scoring men being able to focus their emotional coping better. In these studies, blood pressure is used as a proxy for cardiovascular activity. A study of patients with cardiovascular disease who completed the situational humour response scale found that they were lower scorers than a control group on this measure (Clark, Seidler & Miller, 2001). They also scored more highly on an aggression and hostility scale and laughed less in response to normally funny events in everyday life, suggesting to the authors that a potential protective factor is less apparent in these patients (although the reason might be obvious – they had heart disease), and this affects their emotional response.

Most of the physiological research has focused on the immune system, specifically stress hormones and antibodies. The most commonly studied antibody has been salivary immunoglobulin A (sIgA) because this can easily be extracted from healthy individuals through saliva swabs. Low levels have been associated with the experience of increased stress and frustration. The first study to take measures of this chemical and correlate it with sense of humour found that people scoring low on three of four scales of humour showed a negative correlation between sIgA and the number of daily hassles experienced (Dobbin & Martin, 1988). Forty introductory psychology students from a Canadian university were measured at two points. Many of the correlations the study reported were not statistically significant. The significant correlation was also weak.

Other studies, often with small sample sizes, followed. For example, one study found that exposure to a 60-minute comedy video was associated with a reduction in cortisol (a hormone produced by the body in response to stressors) in 5 participants (the total number in the study was 10). A study exclusively of women found an increase in sIgA production in those who had watched a humorous videotape (Bill Cosby) compared to those who had watched a sad one, which showed lower antibody secretion (Labott, Ahleman, Wolever & Martin, 1990). Lefcourt Davidson-Katz and Kueneman (1990), in a study of the effect of audio and video comedy exposure on sIgA secretion, found the typical pattern: the comedy condition was associated with increases in sIgA after they were watched or listened to. Again, the study, which comprised three experiments, had small samples.

An interesting variant of these studies was published in 2000 by Harrison et al. They examined the effect of watching a funny film, an exciting film (the penalty shoot-out of the Argentina vs. England World Cup game) and a "didactic" film (a maths lesson) on sIgA secretion and cardiovascular activity in 30 undergraduates (note the low numbers, again). The exciting film, as you might expect, had predictable effects on physiological response, producing higher systolic blood pressure and heart rate. The didactic condition produced little significant effect on the measures. And contrary to previous findings, sIgA did not vary between conditions, a finding you would need to interpret cautiously in the context of the number of participants in the study.

So, what can we conclude from this handful of intriguing studies? In short, not much, at least in terms of what they tell us about immunosecretion after exposure to comedy. The problem here is the small sample sizes and an inadequate database on which to draw a conclusion. And what is interesting is that since 2016, no studies have directly examined this relationship according to my search on Google Scholar in the summer of 2020. It is as if the research has dissipated as quickly as it started.

6

THE USES OF COMEDY II: LEARNING, MARKETING AND ADVERTISING

HUMOUR AND LEARNING/EDUCATION

Humour is seen as one of the more desirable characteristics a teacher or instructor can possess, much like the desirability of the trait in a romantic partner discussed earlier. In various surveys, this trait comes among the top among those which students like to see in their teachers. Whether humour works as an instructional tactic, a learning tactic or a remembering tactic, however, is not exactly clear. An excellent review by Powell and Andresen (1985) of the use of humour in teaching and higher education outlined nine ways in which humour might add value in this context: promoting comprehension and retention, creating a positive classroom environment, encouraging student involvement, holding students' attention, fostering cognitive development, managing undesirable behaviour, building self-confidence, enhancing the quality of students' lives and enhancing the quality of teachers' lives.

Some studies have supported some of these proposed ideal outcomes; others have not. All depends on the context of the study, the type of learning, the type of instruction, the type of participant, the type of humour and the time of the study. And, as Ziv (1988) points out, until the early 1980s, although various articles had been written on the importance of humour in education, there was actually very little

DOI: 10.4324/9780429347269-6

research to test any of the ideas about the effects of humour on learning, and of those studies which did try and test some of these ideas, one review found that only one in nine showed a positive effect of humour (Gruner, 1976).

Ziv notes that the contexts involved in these studies were highly artificial. Two studies of students' perceptions found that, across 70 courses, 80% of lecturers used humour at least once in a one-hour lecture (Bryant, Comisky, Crane & Zillmann, 1980) and that 10th-grade students who watched a videotape of an actor playing a teacher were more likely to like and judge as original that teacher who mixed self-disparaging humour with disparagement of others (e.g., students). The study also found that the teacher who disparaged others was judged to be more powerful (Ziv, Gorenstein & Moris, 1986). The teacher not using any humour was perceived as being more systematic. Ziv noted that the former study was never replicated, wondering "if such an abundance of humorous elements in American college teaching does, in fact, exist, or if something funny was happening at the University of Massachusetts." Ziv's study of the use of humour in a one-semester statistics/introductory psychology course found that people allocated to the humour condition performed better in an end-of-term exam. A typical example of the type of humour used in the statistics group was:

> While teaching about means and standard deviations, the teacher projected a slide of a cartoon. It showed an explorer in Africa, talking to a few native children who watch him somewhat surprised. Behind the explorer, and without his being aware of it, is a huge crocodile with a wide-open mouth, ready to swallow him. He, addressing the kids, say "There is no need to be afraid of crocodiles; around here the average length is only about 50 centimetres." One of the children says to another: "This guy had better think about the standard deviations, too."

Which, as far as humour materials in psychology studies go, is quite funny. The finding was explained by the nature of the material. Studies had shown that humour is only effective if the humour is associated with the material tested. Kaplan and Pascoe (1977), for example, gave three versions of a lecture to university students: humour examples related to the lecture's concepts, humour unrelated to the lecture's concepts or a combination. There was no effect of humour on comprehension immediately after the lecture, but six weeks later, those in the humour + concept lecture did recall more of the conceptual material. Ziv's experiment also included humour directly linked to the to-be-examined material. Three to four instances of humour per hour were deemed the "optimal dose", a finding similar to that of Bryant et al.

Given the ability of humour to make very serious situations less serious, it appears to have no effect on test anxiety. The first study of the effect of using humorous items on tests found that these had no effect on performance, regardless of the anxiety level of the participants (Smith, Ascough, Ettinger & Nelson, 1971), a finding that has been replicated (e.g., Perlini, Nenonen & Lind, 1999). The most likely explanation for this is that the situation is too serious for the humour to exert any effect (there's a floor effect) – test performance counts and, therefore, the introduction of humour may be seen as irrelevant, if it is seen at all. Some studies show that humour as an instructional device may have limited benefits – using humorous cartoons to teach students about learning and psychological concepts, for example, was found to be unsuccessful in Özdoğru and McMorris's (2013) study (although students did like the cartoons).

These studies illustrate two aspects of humour research in learning: the first is the perception of the teacher and his or her humour (and whether this is perceived as a positive thing); the other is the actual effect of humour on cognition; that is, does humorous material lead to better retention and understanding than does non-humorous material?

ARE FUNNY INSTRUCTORS DESIRABLE?

The answer to this appears to be universal: yes. The use of humour in the classroom is thought to promote a positive learning environment, lead to better evaluations of the teacher by students and to increase student attention, among other benefits (whether these positive, situational benefits translate to actual learning benefits we'll come back to very soon). Tutors may say funny things, may attempt jokes, may make self-effacing comments and may make derogatory comments about others, amongst other instructional devices deployed. Funny tutors tend to be regarded as extroverted, sociable and likeable (Houser, Cowan & West, 2007). But this perception is mediated by how humour is used and why. For example, students do not tend to value self-deprecating humour, and if the humour is not relevant to the material covered in the class, it has no effect on the students' learning (Frymier, Wanzer & Wojtaszczyk, 2008; Wanzer, Frymier & Irwin, 2010). In one study, Machlev and Karlin (2017) asked 195 students about the type of humour used by their tutor. Their responses could be divided into two categories: relevant and irrelevant humour/use of humour. Both types were associated with student interest, but the relevant use of humour was the most interesting (they also found that the greater the use of irrelevant humour, the less the students' interest in the course). A similar result was found in a large study of 985 German school students which found that course-related humour was associated with the enjoyment of the course and negatively related to boredom and anxiety (Bieg, Grassinger & Dresel, 2017). The use of aggressive humour was not well-received – this was negatively related to enjoyment (which decreased) but positively related to boredom and anxiety (which increased).

The use of humour can also generate other benefits. One study found that the use of appropriate and relevant humour was associated with more rhetorical dissent and with less expressive or vengeful dissent (Sidelinger & Tatum, 2019). The former refers to a student raising issues with the tutor about his or her communication and teaching because it was perceived as being a problem or ineffective; the latter refers to the general expression of dissent and satisfaction about the teaching/tutor to others, not to the tutor; vengeful dissent is an attempt by the student to undermine the tutor, to ruin his or her reputation, damage their credibility and so on by hostile disparagement. Related to this is the perceived homophily between the student and the tutor's humour (remember from the chapter on sex differences that homophily – having similar views and attitudes – is a positive benefit for relationships). West and Martin's (2019) study of 306 students found that when students strongly agreed that their tutor shared a similar humorousness to them, their rating of the tutor's humorousness increased.

A model that has tried to account for the effects of instructional humour on student perception is Wanzer et al.'s (2010) Instructional Humor Processing Theory (IHPT). This argues that relevant humour will improve learning and irrelevant humour will not, the former being achieved because the humour creates a positive environment and increases a student's attention to the to-be-remembered material. This, in turn, leads to a motivation to engage in effortful learning, and it is this that leads to better performance. In order for effortful learning to take place, the student must thoughtfully engaged with the humour-laden material. If the material is positive but distracts from the course content, then this will obviously lead to impaired learning. Tests of the model have not been entirely successful. Bolkan and Goodboy (2015), for example, sought to determine whether the theory could explain student learning in 300 communication studies undergraduates. They found that humour was associated with all the positive things predicted (learning, engagement) but failed to support the idea that for humour to be successful (it has allowed the students to elaborately process the material), it has to increase positive affect and attention. Conversely, Tsukawaki and Imura (2019) found that the students' ability to process material mediated the relationship between relevant humour and student learning. This disagreement aside, however, the conclusion of the studies in the round seems to be that relevant humour can promote student learning by increasing positive affect and attention.

USING COMEDY TO SELL: MARKETING, ADVERTISING AND BRANDING

Think of the adverts that cling to your mind, the ones you never forget and can instantly recall, and they're likely either to be bland (but memorable) or funny (and memorable). Think, for example, of "Every little helps", "As sure as getting it there yourself", "the real thing", "wassup!", "finger-licking good" . . . these are all bland but they are memorable and you will invariably be able to identify the product each is advertising.

The second category – funny and memorable – is also lavishly illustrated. In 2008, the advertising and marketing periodical, *Campaign*, asked its readers to nominate the best advert of all time. Every entry in their top 10 was a comedy. It was topped by the campaign for John West Salmon (you can see the advert here: www.youtube.com/watch?time_continue=1&v=Ys0gj7-VH6A&feature=emb_logo). This featured a John West (the tinned fish people) employee fighting with a bear for a fresh salmon, culminating with the employee kicking the bear in its groin (the bear is obviously a person in a bear costume) and taking the salmon. In second place is the advert for Tango Blackcurrant in which Tango representative Ray Gardner reads a letter to camera from a French exchange student, Sebastian Lloyd, who complains about the new flavour of Tango. Filmed as if it is one complete tracking shot, it culminates in a spectacular crescendo on the white cliffs of Dover with Ray in a boxing ring ranting to a receding overhead helicopter about Sebastian and France, surrounded by crowds of cheering Brits (you can see video here: www.youtube.com/watch?time_continue=9&v=kNDP11XVg94&feature=emb_logo). The source of Brexit can probably be traced back to this one advert.

These are just two of many adverts which use comedy to sell and engender brand awareness and loyalty. There are many others: Joan Collins and Leonard Rossiter and Cinzano Bianco, Heineken's "reaches the parts other beers cannot reach", Gregor Fisher's combed-over photobooth customer in the advert for Hamlet cigars. And humour in adverts is a popular device (the Clio Awards presents gongs for the best use of humour in an advert annually). In the UK, around 36% of TV adverts use humour, with a similar percentage recorded for the United States (31%) (Eisend, 2018). A much older study from the 1990s found that 10% of French and American adverts used humour (Biswas, Olsen & Carlet, 1992), while a later study of print adverts in the United States, China and France found that the use of humour varied between 16% and 24% (Laroche, Nepomuceno, Huang & Richard, 2011). Around 20% of US TV adverts have been found to use humour (Beard, 2005), with Greek television being particularly ticklish – around 60% to 70% of Greek TV adverts were found to have some humour content (Leonidas, Boutsouki & Zotos, 2009). A review of the Superbowl ads in the United States has found a doubling of humorous adverts from 2005 to 2009 (Blackford, Gentry, Harrison & Carlson, 2011), with separate analyses showing that comedic violence has increased even more violently –from 13.6% in 1989 to 84.2% in 2009 (Gulas, Larsen & Coleman, 2009). We'll take another look at the role of violence in comedy and adverts later.

These adverts certainly raise brand awareness – you can probably recall them even now – but whether they increase brand consumption is a separate question for which we have no conclusive data (because companies do not release these data and we really have no control condition with which to compare any commercial success). The research on the effect of comedy in advertising and messaging is small and not especially consistent, with small or patchy effects reported. Probably the first academic study of the use of humour in advertising was that published in 1973 by Sternthal and Craig; it found that humour made people pay more attention to the advert. Apart from the methodological issues that this and subsequent studies raise, there are also some more interesting questions about the effect of the humour and comedy itself: Does it make the brand/product more likeable, does it make the brand/product more memorable, does it help you remember features of the brand/product better or even all three? These are some of the questions Eisend (2009) considered in his review of the literature. He identified several purposes of humour, including increasing attention towards a product, increasing awareness towards it, enhancing the linking of the product and the source of the product, increasing people's positive response to the item and decreasing negative responses.

The review suggests that the effect of humour on comprehension of adverts, or the recall/recognition of adverts, is inconsistent. Our attitudes towards a product, based on its humour, is also complicated, driven by the nature of the humour, how this is presented to us and the type of audience it is intended for. Eisend notes that studies have differed in all of these and that the people most likely to be influenced by humour are young, well-educated and male (many of the studies recruit student participants). There is also the problem of the stimuli themselves in experimental studies – these are often concocted by the experimenter with varying degrees of success. While funny adverts are positively regarded by viewers, it does not necessarily follow that using humour to promote brands may be the most effective way of promoting those brands because it may actually detract from the key brand message (Woltman, Mukherjee & Hoyer, 2004). Few brands build their reputation in this way, and you can clearly identify the ones which do (Red Bull, for example, and, more recently, Pot Noodle). Some research has even found that humour can be detrimental to a product if the advert includes highly threatening humour and ridicules a specific group of people rather than people in general (Warren & McGraw, 2016).

The review concluded that humour can increase the attention and positive feeling expressed towards an advert, but leaves the liking of the advertiser unaffected. It also decreases source credibility and purchase intention but has little effect on comprehension and the purchasing behaviour of consumers. This conclusion rests on two important plinths: audience characteristics and the type of humour stimuli. A follow-up meta-analysis argued that humour was also beneficial to advertising because it decreases the negative conditions surrounding an advert, i.e., the humour distracts from the possibility of the consumer making counter-arguments against the product (Eisend, 2011).

Violence in humorous adverts

A lot of comedy in adverts – and in films, come to that – exploits physical humour, often physical humour involving pain or injury.

Fifty-three per cent of 500 aggressive adverts in one study was found to feature humour (Scharrer, Bergstrom, Paradise & Ren, 2006) with men usually depicted as victims (Gulas, McKeage & Weinberger, 2010). A study of comedy films released between 1951 and 2000 found a sharp increase in comedic violence since 1970, and the feature has been pretty consistent since (McIntosh, Murray, Murray & Manian, 2003). A dominant theme of slapstick humour is its violence: the pratfall, the causing of injury to another, the mirthful witnessing of an accident that leads to harm, etc. One of the most famous, and endlessly repeated scenes, from John Sullivan's majestic *Only Fools and Horses* has the lead character, Del Boy, with his friend Trigger out on the town and wanting to impress some ladies in a swanky London yuppy bistro. Del Boy goes to nonchalantly lean on the bar just after, unbeknownst to him, the barman had lifted the bar flap. Instead of leaning, he falls spectacularly over and disappears behind the bar.

Violence has been defined as "the overt depiction of a credible threat of physical force or the actual use of such force intended to physically harm an animate being or group of beings" (Kunkel et al., 1995). In comedy, it is used to generate laughter rather than fear or intimidation. The paragon of this is the Tom & Jerry cartoons, which routinely utilise violence as a vehicle for mirth; Wile E. Coyote comes a close second, as he usually did.

Despite the appearance of violence in adverts, there is little research on its effectiveness or otherwise as a branding or selling tool. An obvious aim is to increase attention to the advert and to increase the viewers' involvement in a positive way, i.e., a way that is not designed to offend them, which is also a possibility with violent content. As you see with cartoon humour, the violence is literally cartoonish and the excessive physical violence has no real-world consequence. Similarly, with clowning, where a clown may whack another with a mallet (a rubber mallet). There are no consequences, which makes the violence a safe vehicle for delivering a message or entertainment.

(Continued)

The use of violence in comic adverts has been found to be associated with memorability (Brown, Bhadury & Pope, 2010), and some types of viewers seem to find comic adverts with high degrees of violence more humorous than do others, i.e., those who rate themselves as being very masculine (Yoon & Kim, 2014). Yoon (2016) exposed 390 individuals to two visual adverts featuring comic violence (these were actual adverts: Pepsi Max's Love Hearts and Bud Lite's Breakup campaigns). In one version of the beer commercial, a couple is breaking up in a moving car and the woman pushes the man out to the tagline "not too heavy, not too light". This study did something quite interesting in that it measured people's norm beliefs about violence – how likely were they to accept it normally. The higher the norms for violence, the more acceptable these adverts were. A second study found similar results for the adverts with low and high violence – these people held more positive attitudes towards violent ads.

HUMOUR AND PUBLIC HEALTH CAMPAIGNS

Some researchers have argued that in order to get across an important or serious message, humour can be used to help convey this message effectively. The reasoning is that humour makes the underlying message (or content) more palatable and more memorable, and a number of studies have suggested positive, persuasive benefits of humour on political communication and sexual health practice (Moyer-Guse, Mahood & Brookes, 2011). Blanc and Brigaud (2014) sought to discover whether humour would lead to better recall of a public health message by asking people to view print adverts about alcohol use, tobacco use and obesity with or without humour content. To give you an example from one of these, the alcohol advert featured a close-up of a bottle of beer and, in the humour condition, was accompanied by the caption "Drinking can cause memory loss or, worse, memory loss" (the non-humour condition featured the rather more po-faced: "Alcohol is responsible for around 10,000 cancer deaths a year"). They found that people paid more attention to the humorous ads, found them more convincing and recognised them better in a later memory test.

A similar study addressed whether humour could leaven the effect of a threatening message and make it more acceptable. Hendriks and Janssen (2018) examined whether humour could enhance the effectiveness of "fear appeals" – those campaigns which are designed to make you engage in less of a behaviour because the behaviour is undesirable and the engagement in this behaviour can lead to terrible consequences. Fear appeals can sometimes produce defensive behaviour in that people ignore or avoid them (Brown & Locker, 2009). Humour might lead to greater message persuasiveness if the ad is very threatening. Men and women also seem to respond differently to these messages, with men responding to fear appeals that are laced with humour more positively than do women (Madden & Weinberger, 1982). More masculine men are also more likely to express an intention to wear a condom if a condom advert was humorous (Conway & Dubé, 2002).

Hendricks and Janssen exposed men and women to two different poster adverts: one on the dangers of excessive alcohol consumption and another on the negative consequences of caffeine ingestion. For example, the poster would feature a man lying on the floor with a terrible statistic about the effect of alcohol consumption on health. In the humorous, high-threat condition, the tag line appeared as "his funeral was a week later" and the outline of his body was made with cans of beer. In the non-humorous condition, he just lay next to some beer bottles (the no-threat condition did not include the tag line). There was little effect of the humour on attitude towards the message, its believability, on participants' attitudes to binge-drinking or intention to engage in binge-drinking. Similar "marginal" (i.e., statistically non-significant) results were reported for the study using the caffeine advert.

CONCLUSION

In the domains of persuasion and learning, the evidence of humour and comedy's efficacy is mixed but does indicate that humour, if judiciously applied, can lead to a better learning environment and to better learning (although it does little to reduce the anxiety produced by examinations). There is very little good research on the use of humour and comedy on advertising (despite the use of comedy in adverts): most studies suggest that it does exert a positive effect on brand attitudes and awareness.

7

FUNNY BONES (AND BRAIN AND BODY)

THE ANATOMY OF LAUGHTER

Everything starts with the brain, even laughter and comedy. Laughter, like speech and screaming, is a vocal act which recruits the vocal tract, which is under control of the voice/motor areas of the brain. It also involves the activation of the diaphragm and the intercostal muscles in the chest – it is the control of these that allows us to measure out our speech and control what we say and how. When we laugh, there are large contractions in the intercostal muscles. One model of vocal control argues that we have two systems in the brain which mediate spontaneous vocalisation (midline motor regions) and learned vocalisation (lateral motor regions). This is the dual-pathway model of vocalisation, one pathway of which is involved in very precise control of laryngeal activity, labial/lingual movement and airflow from the lungs in order to produce speech. It is fair to say, however, that most research focuses on the what of speech (words, syllables) than the how (the vocal/motor cortex/subcortical apparatus necessary to produce all of these). The former is easier to study.

Pisanski, Cartei, McGettigan, Raine and Reby (2016) analysed these systems in their paper on voice modulation and one of the sections focuses on laughter. For example, they report that spontaneous laughter tends to be longer, made up of shorter calls and is of higher

DOI: 10.4324/9780429347269-7

frequency than is voluntary laughter. They note that the hypothalamus has been implicated in spontaneous laughter and the anterior cingulate cortex in the frontal lobe has been implicated in voluntary laughter and in the suppression of laughter during tickling.

PATHOLOGICAL LAUGHTER

Some people can't stop themselves from laughing, and they are an unusual group. What makes them unusual is not that they're tickled by the coarse cross-dressing shenanigans of *Mrs Brown's Boys* or French and Saunders's lardy pub drinkers, nor by the docent culture clash of *Mind Your Language*, nor even by the effete farcical comedies of manners in Wodehouse or Congreve or the domestic, more prosaic equivalent in Ayckbourn and *The Office*. What makes them unusual is that they have a physical condition or illness – frequently, brain injury – which results in the involuntary, affect-less production of laughter, so-called "pathological laughter".

There have been other names for this, too, including "involuntary laughter", "pseudobulbar affect", "dysprosopoeia", "sham mirth" and "emotional incontinence" (Wild, Rodden, Grodd & Ruch, 2003). Some people with brain injury do report involuntary laughter accompanied by relevant affect (they experience mirth and enjoyment). But, by and large, those who express "pathological laughter" do not enjoy the experience. It is purely a motor act. It's just that the motor act is one we associate with pleasant experiences. A recent, well-known fictional example is the film, *Joker*, whose eponymous anti-hero expresses involuntary, affectless laughter. Who are these individuals, and why do they produce this laughter devoid of any emotional meaning? Are there real-life Jokers?

There are two very good reviews of the role of brain injury and illness in pathological laughter. The first is a book chapter by Poeck published in 1969, the first proper summary of studies examining involuntary laughter and brain injury; the second, and slightly more recent, is that of Wild et al. (2003) which is a comprehensive account (up to the date of publication).

What made Poeck's summary important was its classification of the different causes of pathological laughter. He identified three categories: motor neuron disease, pseudobulbar paralysis and motor disorders involving specific neuron types; a rare condition he called "fou rire prodromique"; and epilepsy. These are all causes of pathological laughter, but there are also non-pathological causes of laughter such as nitrous oxide (laughing gas) inhalation and direct brain stimulation (which we'll come back to later). To be classed as pathological, Poeck concluded that the behaviour arises from non-specific stimuli, is not accompanied by a change in affect or mood and is involuntary.

Poeck's third cause, epilepsy, is particularly interesting because there are some epileptic seizures whose primary symptom is laughter, a condition called gelastic epilepsy. Wild et al. note that although the laughter can seem normal, more often than not the type of laughter heard (and seen) in gelastic seizures tends to be stilted and unnatural. Some individuals experience mirth, some don't. Much of the epilepsy work involving the brain is undertaken using electroencephalography (measuring electrical activity from the scalp usually), but the studies which have attempted to localise the source of the defect have identified the hypothalamus and malformations in the area (hamartomas) and pathology of parts of the frontal and temporal lobes (the poles) as being most frequently involved, especially the hypothalamus. Why? One explanation may be that the tumours create excitatory effects resulting in abnormal electrical activation which spreads to the brainstem and the limbic system.

Fou rire prodromique was a condition described by MC Fere in 1903 and is rare. Pathological laughter occurs as one of the first symptoms of ischaemia (or lack of blood flow to the brain, i.e., a stroke). Wild et al. note that the early symptoms are uncontrollable laughter, which can last up to 30 minutes, and may include giggling or crying before the patient exhibits the typical symptoms of a stroke such as paralysis on one side of the body or inability to produce speech (aphasia). The areas of injury associated with the abnormality include a part of the brainstem (pons) and areas of the limbic system (left parahipppocampal gyrus, left thalamus, amygdala or hippocampus).

One mechanism for the abnormality may be that inhibitory neurons in these areas are injured, which results in the involuntary behaviour. Other cases of pathological laughter in stroke have been reported, one of the earliest by Wilson (1924), who described one patient who would laugh at news reports of war – the more solemn the reports, the greater the laughter.

The stimuli causing the laughter can be as trivial as they are irrelevant. Some patients are also aware of the inappropriateness of the laughter, and often the laughter is followed by crying. As might be becoming clear, these patients do not experience much, if any, joy from behaving in this way, which suggests that the pathological laughter is a motor disorder. One study which examined normal and abnormal laughter in the same individuals found that there were some physiognomic signals that distinguished between the two – pathological laughter resulted in more frowning (Tanaka & Sumitsuji, 1991).

The brain regions implicated in pathological laughter are the frontal lobes and the brainstem. Wilson (1924) reported patients expressing pathological laughter had tumours in the pons and tegmentum. Later studies reported abnormalities in other parts of the brainstem. A study of 49 patients with lesions to the paramedial pontine area of the brainstem found that when injury was to the paramedial basal area, patients showed pathological laughter (Kataoka, Hori, Shirakawa & Hirose, 1997). The neurotransmitters dopamine and serotonin might also be involved, as laughter symptoms seem to be reduced with the administration of certain anti-depressants.

STIMULATING THE BRAIN

A more experimental approach to studying the role of the brain in laughter has been to stimulate electrically its various regions and observe the outcome on behaviour. There's a Gary Larson cartoon in which a group of surgeons is surrounding a patient in an operating theatre. You can see the patient's leg in the air and one of the surgeons exclaims, "Whoa! That was a good one! Try it Hobbs – just poke his brain right where my finger is!" Electrical stimulation of the human brain was pioneered by Wilder Penfield in the 1930s and 1940s – it is Penfield's work that led to the well-known motor homunculus showing how much of the brain is devoted to the movement of particular body parts, but it is a technique that is much older than that. The first experimental demonstration of localisation of function in the brain, for example, was conducted on a dressing table in 1870 when Fritsch and Hitzig electrically stimulated parts of a dog's cortex and found that stimulation of different areas led to movement in different limbs and body parts.

Because the procedure is invasive, studies using electrical stimulation are conducted on patients and, in the area of laughter, these patients tend to be those who suffer from epilepsy and are undergoing surgery to alleviate their symptoms. Using this technique, researchers have found that laughter can be elicited from stimulation of the insula, the left basal temporal lobe, the rostral part of the cingulate cortex (10 patients out of 57 in one study), the inferior and superior frontal cortex and the frontal operculum. Almost all areas were associated with motor expressions of laughter and mirth. Most studies found that laughter was elicited by stimulation on the left side, but right-sided production has also been reported.

The difficulty in interpreting these studies, apart from the nature of the participants, is the sample size (small) and the often-questionable methodology such studies employ. No study appears to have considered a double-blind protocol in which the researcher is not aware of the hypothesis being tested.

Overall, pathological and stimulation studies of laughter suggest that there may be separate regions or systems in the brainstem (specifically, the pons and mesencephalon) which mediate emotional laughter and non-emotional laughter and that these regions may be dorsal and ventral regions, respectively, so lesions to the dorsal part lead to impairments in the first and ventral lesions lead to impairments in the second. Early theories of laughter and the brain had suggested that the hypothalamus and diencephalic regions were important for the generation of laughter with an affective (felt) component (e.g., Davison & Kelman, 1939). Others implicated the brainstem in the coordination of the motor aspects of laughter (as Wilson and Poeck had, but the latter suggested that subcortical regions would also be involved in pathological laughter). Both regions are likely to be involved: the brainstem and hypothalamus. Invasive ways of studying smiling and laughter are problematic because movement can contaminate recordings of brain activity: the motor activity is so gross that it is difficult to determine which region of the brain is involved in facial expression, vocalisation, respiration, thoracic movement, shoulder heaving and all the other physical features of the behaviour.

PERCEPTION OF LAUGHTER

Laughter, as you saw in Chapter 1, can be classified into different categories, each with their distinctive acoustic features and perceptions of intention. Sarcastic laughter can be distinguished from joyous laughter, which can be distinguished from the laughter generated by tickling and so on. Each of these seems to be associated with activation in different brain areas. Szameitat et al. (2010), for example, found that perceived laughter that was classed as socially complex was associated with activation in the anterior rostral mediofrontal cortex, whereas Szameitat et al. (2009) found that laughter produced by tickling was associated with activation in the auditory association cortex. Activation in the auditory cortex seems to be greater to laughter than to speech stimuli, which suggests that it may be more sensitive to the acoustic properties of what it processes. Wildgruber et al. (2013) were interested in whether connections between regions would be more or less activated during the perception of different types of laughter. In a study of 18 participants (yes, those low numbers again), they found that laughter associated with tickling, which was also associated with changes in the connections between the prefrontal cortex and the auditory association areas, whereas socially meaningful laughter was associated with increases in activation in the connections between a range of brain regions known to be involved in laughter: these include the auditory association cortices, the right dorsolateral prefrontal cortex and the visual association cortex. Some people also respond to laughter negatively – these are the people who experience gelotophobia (which you read about earlier). A direct study of gelotophobes by Chan (2016) found that this group showed less activation in specific brain regions (the ventral mesocorticolimbic system) than did non-gelotophobes when listening to hostile and non-hostile jokes.

BRAIN INJURY AND APPRECIATION OF HUMOUR AND COMEDY

According to one of neuroscience's pioneers, the key to modern neuroscience is the localisation of function in the brain: to try and identify and understand which region is responsible for what function. Of course, it is more complicated than that. Damage or activation in a part of the brain which is associated with a deficit or an anomaly or a dysfunction does not necessarily mean that this part is responsible for the function disrupted or altered. Regions do not operate in isolation; they are not neural islands. But from the 1960s to the 1990s, much of the work on understanding what the brain did focused on whether function could be localised in specific sides (hemispheres) or regions of the brain, and the primary source of these endeavours was patients with brain injury, the source material of many of psychology's theories about brain function and behaviour. One of the functions studied was humour appreciation – understanding or getting a joke or cartoon – and early studies were pretty much unanimous in concluding that the right hemisphere was more important than the left. Lesions to the left hemisphere were important to the extent that jokes and comedy might involve language, which is primarily a function undertaken by parts of the left hemisphere in most people, and so people with injury to the left hemisphere leading to aphasia (an inability to produce or comprehend speech) may not be able to comprehend the linguistic nature of jokes.

The earliest systematic study of the effect of brain injury on humour appreciation was Gardner, Albert and Weintraub's (1975). This found that brain injury impaired patients' ability to distinguish between funny and unfunny cartoons but did not find that damage to one side had more of an effect than the other. Brownell, Michel, Powelson and Gardner (1983) studied 12 patients with right hemisphere lesions and 12 undamaged controls and presented participants with 16 jokes with the punchlines missing. Participants had to select the correct punchline from options including the correct one, a non sequitur, a neutral one and one with a sad ending. The right-sided patients were not only poorer at selecting the correct punchline, they were more likely to choose the non sequitur, suggesting to the authors that these patients had difficulty integrating information into a meaningful whole. Similar studies of right hemisphere injury followed, indicating that these patients had more difficulty in understanding humour whether this humour was delivered via a joke or via cartoon. Some of these studies did not investigate left hemisphere lesions.

A study that did also looked at the role of the frontal lobe specifically because we know that this lobe in the brain allows us to integrate information and to monitor the environment for change. It is a huge part of the brain – around a third of the cortex – and so is involved in all manner of functions from regulating impulsivity, to olfactory identification, to speech and motor movement (it contains the premotor cortex), to eye movement and planning. Shammi and Stuss (1999) found that patients with right frontal lesions were poorer at discriminating between funny and unfunny cartoons and were also less expressive when they saw the funny cartoons than were patients with left frontal lesions. Left-based lesions are generally associated with a failure to understand language – it is not that patients are not able to appreciate humour (they can), but they have difficulty in appreciating humour that involves ambiguous or complex language.

The next section shifts the focus from brain injury to healthy brains. Since the late 1980s, researchers have been able to harness the ostensible benefits of neuroimaging (via scanners such as positron emission tomography [PET] or functional magnetic resonance imaging [fMRI] and magnetoencephalography [MEG]) to examine how the uninjured brain responds to comedy. They have even been able to study very granular responses such as people's responses to

The Simpsons and *Seinfeld*. One group was able to monitor participants' understanding of a joke.

NEUROIMAGING AND THE APPRECIATION OF COMEDY

To understand how the brain processes comedy, researchers have taken two routes: the psychophysiological (event-related potentials [ERPs]) and the neurophysiological (imaging). The former examines the how of humour processing (such as when a joke is "got" or what happens when a person reads a punchline); the latter examines where humour processing occurs, to the extent that neuroimaging can do this. ERPs are recordings of the brain's electrical response to the presentation of stimuli over time. These responses are then averaged, and researchers can observe whether any changes occurred in brain activity over periods of milliseconds. In a basic sensory experiment – where people listen to tones or see flashes of light, for example – a trough at 100 ms (N100) and a peak at 200 ms (P200) is usually observed, reflecting the point at which early sensory processing occurs in the brain. If the participant needs to make a decision, such as counting the number of low tones in a series of high and low tones where there are always fewer low tones, a positive peak at 300 ms occurs, and this is thought to reflect decision-making or context-updating. In humour studies, the ERP that is affected is the N400, a negative peak at 400 ms, which is often elicited when people read sentences with ambiguous endings. The N400 follows the resolution of the ambiguous ending – participants are given the whole sentence apart from the last key word and are then presented with the key word. When people hear or read funny jokes or see funny cartoons, the N400 is larger than it is for unfunny material (Coulson & Kutas, 2001; Feng, Chan & Chen, 2014). In humour, this change might reflect a resolution of the ambiguity in the material or it might reflect a surprise at the ending. Later peaks occurring after 500 ms have been thought to reflect a person trying to resolve the ambiguity in the joke or cartoon (Du et al., 2013).

The first neuroimaging study (fMRI) of humour was published in 2001. Goel and Dolan compared brain activation elicited by jokes that participants found funny or unfunny and found that the ventral medial prefrontal cortex and both sides of the cerebellum were active during the jokes participants found funny. The next major study reported that areas of the subcortex (particularly the nucleus accumbens) and cortex (especially the frontotemporal areas) interacted to allow humour appreciation (Mobbs, Greicius, Abdel-Azim, Menon & Reiss, 2003). When participants viewed cartoons they thought were funny, activation was higher in the left temporo-occipital junction, inferior frontal gyrus and temporal pole. Mobbs et al. argued that the temporo-occipital junction and the fusiform gyrus were the regions which processed surprise and ambiguity resolution.

A study comparing differences between visual and verbal humour found that different brain areas were activated during each (Watson, Matthews & Allman, 2007). As you might predict, verbal humour activated language regions in the brain (such as the left temporal lobe), whereas visual material was associated with activity in the parts of the cortex which process visual stimuli (extrastriate areas such as V1 and V2). Both types of material were associated with activation in the nucleus accumbens and the amygdala. The amygdala appears to be a structure that is surprisingly more involved than most in our positive response to comedy material, with a number of studies finding increased activation in this structure to material we find funny. The anterior cingulate cortex and the insula were also activated by the humorous stimuli in Watson et al.'s study. In a study where 24 women were asked to inhibit their response to visual "jokes" (e.g., a snail mounting a tape dispenser which looks like a snail) – a process called emotional suppression – Korb et al. (2012) found that late positive ERPs were larger to the joke than non-joke conditions when participants did not inhibit their mirth but there were no differences in these ERPs when people suppressed mirth (neither did participants in this condition find the jokes less funny, which is an unusual result given the material we discussed in Chapter 1).

The majority of the imaging studies has focused on the incongruity resolution model of humour appreciation and sought to determine whether different regions of the brain become more or less active during the set-up of a joke (comprehension) and during its resolution. Bartolo, Benuzzi, Nocetti, Baraldi and Nichelli (2006) asked 21 adults to watch and rate cartoons made of two images (the first the set-up, the second the punchline) in an fMRI study. Once the second of the images had been presented, participants rated the cartoon for funniness. They were instructed not to laugh while inside the scanner. The study found that activation was higher in the right inferior frontal gyrus, left superior temporal gyrus, left middle temporal gyrus and left cerebellum when the jokes were judged to be funny. The authors suggest that this activation reflects participants' ability to attribute intention in the cartoon and to resolve ambiguity. Funniness of the joke correlated positively with activity in the (left) amygdala.

Another study explored whether people's responses would differ to verbal jokes with ambiguous words, jokes with unambiguous words and sentences that were unfunny but included ambiguous words (Bekinschtein, Davis, Rodd & Owen, 2011). Regions were involved in the processing of ambiguous aspects of language (left inferior temporal gyrus and left inferior frontal gyrus) and others involved in the processing of humorous sentences – the same regions plus the temporoparietal junction. Hearing jokes was associated with increased activation in different regions, including the amygdala, ventral striatum and midbrain, and this activation correlated positively with ratings of the material's funniness.

Some studies have taken this approach a little further and divided the joke processing into separate components: comprehension and elaboration. Comprehension involves making sense of the joke and resolving any ambiguity; elaboration involves the generation of inferences about people or objects in the joke/cartoon and which make it funny. This is what results in amusement or enjoyment of the material. Moran, Wig, Adams Jr, Janata and Kelley (2004), for example, had participants watch clips from *The Simpsons* and *Seinfeld* and, cleverly, estimated when detection/comprehension and appreciation occurred by using the laughter responses from the shows – the laughter indicated when the joke was "got", i.e., appreciated. They found that during the detection phase of processing, activation was higher in the left inferior frontal and posterior temporal cortex, whereas the appreciation part was associated with activation in both sides of the amygdala and insula. Chan, Chou, Chen and Liang (2012) developed this technique further and adopted a "garden path" approach to joke presentation where a 110- to 130-character set-up was followed by a 15- to 30-character punchline that was funny or not funny or which required ambiguity resolution without accompanying amusement. They found that comprehending the joke/set-up was associated with activation in both sides of the inferior frontal gyri and left superior frontal gyrus, whereas amusement was associated with activation in the amygdala and parahippocampal gyrus (both sides). The same group investigated incongruity resolution in jokes that were funny, unfunny (no incongruity) or nonsensical and found that detecting ambiguity was associated with activation in the right middle temporal gyrus and right medial frontal gyrus. Resolving ambiguity was associated with activation in the left superior frontal gyrus and left inferior parietal lobule (Chan et al., 2013).

The Chan group also published the first fMRI study of response to one-liners, specifically jokes in which the target was the self or others and whether the joke was benign or not (Chan et al., 2018). In a study of 42 Mandarin speakers, they found that connections between the temporal pole and the frontal areas of the brain were associated with appreciation of self-directed humour and the temporo-parietal junction and frontal area connectivity was associated with other-directed jokes. Different regions were active during the benign and non-benign conditions, with the amygdala and the frontal lobe active during the appreciation of the former and the nucleus accumbens and temporal area active during the latter.

A unique fMRI study examined the brain's response to manga cartoons as frames of a funny or unfunny cartoon were presented to participants one at a time – four frames in all (Osaka, Yaoi, Minamoto & Osaka, 2014). They found changes in activation in a group of 15 participants to each frame. The second frame (which they called the development scene) was associated with activation in the temporoparietal junction and the third with activation in the temporal and frontal cortex. The fourth frame (the punchline) was associated with increased activation in the medial prefrontal cortex and cerebellum. Shibata, Terasawa and Umeda (2014) also found that funny punchlines were associated with activation in the inferior frontal gyrus, middle temporal gyrus and other language areas during comprehension and other regions during appreciation. Bringing two techniques together – MEG and ERP – to investigate the time course of ambiguity resolution, Marinkovic et al. (2011) presented participants with sentences (questions) where the replies were logical, nonsensical or funny ("How do you become an executioner? Just axe"). They identified two stages of spatiotemporal activation: one in the bilateral temporal lobes and left inferior prefrontal cortex that was active during semantic analysis and a second which seemed to reflect interpretation and integration of lexical information, which recruited the right dorsolateral and parts of the left prefrontal cortex. The late-going positive waves described earlier were seen when people were exposed to the funny punchline. The study was yet another exploring the garden path nature of joke appreciation.

Returning to the amygdala, two studies have found activation in this structure during ambiguity resolution and that this activation might depend on specific personality characteristics. Nakamura et al. (2018) found that incongruity resolution was associated with increased activation in the left amygdala and with increased amusement, whereas Berger, Bitsch, Nagels, Straube and Falkenberg (2018) found increased activation in connections between the typical humour detection/comprehension areas described in this section and the amygdala and insula and that these connections were mediated by neuroticism and extraversion in 19 participants. Funniness ratings of the cartoons were associated with activation in the right amygdala and left insula, with extraversion associated with modulating (increasing) the connectivity between the amygdala and caudate nucleus, suggesting to the authors that extroverts are more sensitive to the rewarding aspects of humour. Neuroticism was associated with increased connectivity between the right amygdala and the right middle and inferior temporal gyrus, suggesting to the authors that neurotic individuals are more sensitive to the cognitive aspects of humour (and may laugh and smile less).

Finally, given some of the sex differences in response to, and in production of, humour and comedy, very few imaging studies have compared the responses of men and women. One has found that men and women showed similar activation in brain regions during the rating of funny verbal and non-verbal material (the temporal-occipital junction, inferior frontal gyrus and temporal pole), with women showing greater activation of the left prefrontal cortex and nucleus accumbens (Azim, Mobbs, Jo, Memon & Reiss, 2005).

CONCLUSION

Are there any conclusions we can draw about how the brain allows us to process comedy and humour? The first observation we can make is that these studies have been fairly restricted in terms of the processes and protocols they have adopted – many have sought to explore the processes involved in incongruity resolution. Most have done this via jokes or cartoons; very few have done so via moving image (such as TV shows or comedy film clips). Above and beyond some quotidian conclusions – such as language areas of the brain are more active during verbal humour and visual areas are more active during visual humour – studies do seem to converge on three tentative conclusions: (1) the temporo-parietal junction (including the inferior frontal and temporal gyrus) is involved in humour comprehension; (2) subcortical areas, including the amygdala, nucleus accumbens, insula and ventral striatum, are involved in humour appreciation; and (3) activation in the amygdala is observed when people find material funny. There is a fourth conclusion and that is this: there is great variability between neuroimaging studies, not simply in their methodology, samples and materials (which is problematic enough) but in the regions in which they report activation or no activation.

CURTAIN FALLS – GET OFF THE STAGE

And this, after seven chapters and our review of the brain in comedy, is where our revels end.

I hope you've enjoyed this brisk canter through the psychology of comedy and that you've discovered a lot you did not already know. There was much that I had to cull from the book for space – material on performers' personalities; the effect of drinking on the perception of comedy; the effect of a good mood on gambling; emotional intelligence and sense of humour; the role of genetics in humour, a terrific knock-knock joke . . . more than enough for another book. But now I'm using up more words and that won't do.

Therefore, I'll leave some of the last to George Santayana. In *The Sense of Beauty* (1896), he wrote: "there is nothing in comedy that is not delightful except, perhaps, the moment when it is over".

You've been a lovely audience. Goodnight and may your god go with you.

REFERENCES

Allport, G. W. (1960). The open system in personality theory. *The Journal of Abnormal and Social Psychology*, 61(3), 301.

Ando, V., Claridge, G., & Clark, K. (2014). Psychotic traits in comedians. *The British Journal of Psychiatry*, 204(5), 341–345.

Apatow, J. (2015). *Sick in the head: Conversations about life and comedy*. New York: Random House.

Apostolou, M., & Christoforou, C. (2020, in press). The art of flirting: What are the traits that make it effective? *Personality and Individual Differences*, 158, 109866.

Apter, M. J. (1982). *The experience of motivation: The theory of psychological reversals*. New York: Academic Press.

Apter, M. J. (1991). A structural phenomenology of stress. *Stress and Anxiety*, 13, 13–22.

Apter, M. J., & Smith, K. C. P. (1977). Humour and the theory of psychological reversals. In A. Chapman & H. Foot (Eds.), *It's a funny thing, humour*-International conference on humour & laughter (pp. 95–100).

Averill, J. R. (1969). Autonomic response patterns during sadness and mirth. *Psychophysiology*, 5(4), 399–414.

Azim, E., Mobbs, D., Jo, B., Menon, V., & Reiss, A. L. (2005). Sex differences in brain activation elicited by humor. *Proceedings of the National Academy of Sciences*, 102(45), 16496–16501.

Bachorowski, J. A., Smoski, M. J., & Owren, M. J. (2001). The acoustic features of human laughter. *The Journal of the Acoustical Society of America, 110*(3), 1581–1597.

Bartolo, A., Benuzzi, F., Nocetti, L., Baraldi, P., & Nichelli, P. (2006). Humor comprehension and appreciation: AN FMRI study. *Journal of Cognitive Neuroscience, 18*(11), 1789–1798.

Beard, F. K. (2005). One hundred years of humor in American advertising. *Journal of Macromarketing, 25*(1), 54–65.

Bekinschtein, T. A., Davis, M. H., Rodd, J. M., & Owen, A. M. (2011). Why clowns taste funny: The relationship between humor and semantic ambiguity. *Journal of Neuroscience, 31*(26), 9665–9671.

Berger, P., Bitsch, F., Nagels, A., Straube, B., & Falkenberg, I. (2018). Personality modulates amygdala and insula connectivity during humor appreciation: An event-related fMRI study. *Social Neuroscience, 13*(6), 756–768.

Bergson, H. (1911). *Laughter: An essay on the meaning of the comic.* Los Angeles: Green Integer.

Berlyne, D. E. (1960). *Conflict, arousal, and curiosity.* New York: McGraw-Hill.

Berlyne, D. E. (1969). Arousal, reward and learning. *Annals of the New York Academy of Sciences, 159*(3), 1059–1070.

Berlyne, D. E. (1972). Humor and its kin. In J. H. Goldstein & P. McGhee (Eds.), *The psychology of humor: Theoretical perspectives and empirical issues.* Amsterdam: Elsevier.

Bieg, S., Grassinger, R., & Dresel, M. (2017). Humor as a magic bullet? Associations of different teacher humor types with student emotions. *Learning and Individual Differences, 56*, 24–33.

Biswas, A., Olsen, J. E., & Carlet, V. (1992). A comparison of print advertisements from the United States and France. *Journal of Advertising, 21*(4), 73–81.

Bitterly, T. B., Brooks, A. W., & Schweitzer, M. E. (2017). Risky business: When humor increases and decreases status. *Journal of Personality and Social Psychology, 112*(3), 431.

Blackford, B. J., Gentry, J., Harrison, R. L., & Carlson, L. (2011). The prevalence and influence of the combination of humor and violence in Super Bowl commercials. *Journal of Advertising, 40*(4), 123–134.

Blanc, N., & Brigaud, E. (2014). Humor in print health advertisements: Enhanced attention, privileged recognition, and persuasiveness of preventive messages. *Health Communication, 29*(7), 669–677.

Blanchard, D. C., Graczyk, B., & Blanchard, R. J. (1986). Differential reactions of men and women to realism, physical damage, and emotionality in violent films. *Aggressive Behavior*, 12(1), 45–55.

Boerner, M., Joseph, S., & Murphy, D. (2017). The association between sense of humor and trauma-related mental health outcomes: Two exploratory studies. *Journal of Loss and Trauma*, 22(5), 440–452.

Bolkan, S., & Goodboy, A. K. (2015). Exploratory theoretical tests of the instructor humor–student learning link. *Communication Education*, 64(1), 45–64.

Brauer, K., & Proyer, R. T. (2018). To love and laugh: Testing actor-, partner-, and similarity effects of dispositions towards ridicule and being laughed at on relationship satisfaction. *Journal of Research in Personality*, 76, 165–176.

Brauer, K., Proyer, R. T., & Ruch, W. (2019). Extending the study of gelotophobia, gelotophilia, and katagelasticism in romantic life toward romantic attachment. *Journal of Individual Differences*, 41(2), 86–100.

Bressler, E. R., & Balshine, S. (2006). The influence of humor on desirability. *Evolution and Human Behavior*, 27(1), 29–39.

Brown, M. R., Bhadury, R. K., & Pope, N. K. L. (2010). The impact of comedic violence on viral advertising effectiveness. *Journal of Advertising*, 39(1), 49–66.

Brown, S., & Locker, E. (2009). Defensive responses to an emotive anti-alcohol message. *Psychology and Health*, 24(5), 517–528.

Brownell, H. H., Michel, D., Powelson, J., & Gardner, H. (1983). Surprise but not coherence: Sensitivity to verbal humor in right-hemisphere patients. *Brain and Language*, 18(1), 20–27.

Bryant, G. A., & Aktipis, C. A. (2014). The animal nature of spontaneous human laughter. *Evolution and Human Behavior*, 35(4), 327–335.

Bryant, G. A., Fessler, D. M., Fusaroli, R., Clint, E., Aarøe, L., Apicella, C. L., . . . De Smet, D. (2016). Detecting affiliation in colaughter across 24 societies. *Proceedings of the National Academy of Sciences*, 113(17), 4682–4687.

Bryant, G. A., Fessler, D. M., Fusaroli, R., Clint, E., Amir, D., Chávez, B., . . . Fux, M. (2018). The perception of spontaneous and volitional laughter across 21 societies. *Psychological Science*, 29(9), 1515–1525.

Bryant, J., Comisky, P. W., Crane, J. S., & Zillmann, D. (1980). Relationship between college teachers' use of humor in the classroom and students' evaluations of their teachers. *Journal of Educational Psychology*, 72(4), 511.

Bucaria, C., & Barra, L. (2016). *Taboo comedy: Television and controversial humour*. Springer.

Buijzen, M., & Valkenburg, P. M. (2004). Developing a typology of humor in audiovisual media. *Media Psychology*, 6(2), 147–167.

Buss, D. M. (1988). The evolution of human intrasexual competition: Tactics of mate attraction. *Journal of Personality and Social Psychology*, 54(4), 616.

Butcher, J., & Whissell, C. (1984). Laughter as a function of audience size, sex of the audience, and segments of the short film "Duck Soup". *Perceptual and Motor Skills*, 59(3), 949–950.

Butland, M. J., & Ivy, D. K. (1990). The effects of biological sex and egalitarianism on humor appreciation: Replication and extension. *Journal of Social Behavior and Personality*, 5(4), 353.

Butzer, B., & Kuiper, N. A. (2008). Humor use in romantic relationships: The effects of relationship satisfaction and pleasant versus conflict situations. *The Journal of Psychology*, 142(3), 245–260.

Caird, S., & Martin, R. A. (2014). Relationship-focused humor styles and relationship satisfaction in dating couples: A repeated-measures design. *Humor*, 27(2), 227–247.

Campbell, L., & Moroz, S. (2014). Humour use between spouses and positive and negative interpersonal behaviours during conflict. *Europe's Journal of Psychology*, 10(3), 532–542.

Cann, A., & Cann, A. T. (2013). Humor styles, risk perceptions, and risky behavioral choices in college students. *Humor*, 26(4), 595–608.

Cann, A., & Collette, C. (2014). Sense of humor, stable affect, and psychological well-being. *Europe's Journal of Psychology*, 10(3), 464–479.

Cann, A., Davis, H. B., & Zapata, C. L. (2011). Humor styles and relationship satisfaction in dating couples: Perceived versus self-reported humor styles as predictors of satisfaction. *Humor*, 24(1), 1–20.

Cantor, J. R. (1976). What is funny to whom? The role of gender. *Journal of Communication*. 26(3), 164–172.

Carlson, E. R. (1966). The affective tone of psychology. *The Journal of General Psychology*, 75(1), 65–78.

Carlsson, K., Petrovic, P., Skare, S., Petersson, K. M., & Ingvar, M. (2000). Tickling expectations: Neural processing in anticipation of a sensory stimulus. *Journal of Cognitive Neuroscience*, 12(4), 691–703.

Chan, Y. C. (2016). Neural correlates of deficits in humor appreciation in Gelotophobics. *Scientific Reports*, 6, 34580.

Chan, Y. C., Chou, T. L., Chen, H. C., & Liang, K. C. (2012). Segregating the comprehension and elaboration processing of verbal jokes: An fMRI study. *Neuroimage*, 61(4), 899–906.

Chan, Y. C., Chou, T. L., Chen, H. C., Yeh, Y. C., Lavallee, J. P., Liang, K. C., & Chang, K. E. (2013). Towards a neural circuit model of verbal humor processing: An fMRI study of the neural substrates of incongruity detection and resolution. *Neuroimage*, 66, 169–176.

Chan, Y. C., Hsu, W. C., Liao, Y. J., Chen, H. C., Tu, C. H., & Wu, C. L. (2018). Appreciation of different styles of humor: An fMRI study. *Scientific Reports*, 8(1), 1–12.

Chapman, A. J. (1973). Funniness of jokes, canned laughter and recall performance. *Sociometry*, 569–578.

Chen, G. H., & Martin, R. A. (2007). A comparison of humor styles, coping humor, and mental health between Chinese and Canadian university students. *Humor*, 20(3), 215–234.

Cheng, D., & Wang, L. (2015). Examining the energizing effects of humor: The influence of humor on persistence behavior. *Journal of Business and Psychology*, 30(4), 759–772.

Christensen, A. P., Silvia, P. J., Nusbaum, E. C., & Beaty, R. E. (2018). Clever people: Intelligence and humor production ability. *Psychology of Aesthetics, Creativity, and the Arts*, 12(2), 136.

Clark, A., Seidler, A., & Miller, M. (2001). Inverse association between sense of humor and coronary heart disease. *International Journal of Cardiology*, 80(1), 87–88.

Cogan, R., Cogan, D., Waltz, W., & McCue, M. (1987). Effects of laughter and relaxation on discomfort thresholds. *Journal of Behavioral Medicine*, 10(2), 139–144.

Coles, N. A., Larsen, J. T., & Lench, H. C. (2019). A meta-analysis of the facial feedback literature: Effects of facial feedback on emotional experience are small and variable. *Psychological Bulletin*, 145(6), 610.

Conway, M., & Dubé, L. (2002). Humor in persuasion on threatening topics: Effectiveness is a function of audience sex role orientation. *Personality and Social Psychology Bulletin*, 28(7), 863–873.

Coulson, S., & Kutas, M. (2001). Getting it: Human event-related brain response to jokes in good and poor comprehenders. *Neuroscience Letters*, 316(2), 71–74.

Cupchik, G. C., & Leventhal, H. (1974). Consistency between expressive behavior and the elevation of humorous stimuli: The role of sex and self-observation. *Journal of Personality and Social Psychology*, 30(3), 429.

Curry, O. S., & Dunbar, R. I. (2013). Sharing a joke: The effects of a similar sense of humor on affiliation and altruism. *Evolution and Human Behavior*, 34(2), 125–129.

Damico, S. B., & Purkey, W. W. (1978). Class clowns: A study of middle school students. *American Educational Research Journal*, 15(3), 391–398.

Darwin, C. (1872). *The expression of the emotions in man and animals*. London. J. Murray.

Davison, C., & Kelman, H. (1939). Pathologic laughing and crying. *Archives of Neurology & Psychiatry*, 42(4), 595–643.

Dezecache, G., & Dunbar, R. I. (2012). Sharing the joke: The size of natural laughter groups. *Evolution and Human Behavior*, 33(6), 775–779.

Dionigi, A., & Canestrari, C. (2018). The use of humor by therapists and clients in cognitive therapy. *The European Journal of Humour Research*, 6(3), 50–67.

Dobbin, J. P., & Martin, R. A. (1988). Telic versus paratelic dominance: Personality moderator of biochemical responses to stress. In *Advances in psychology* (Vol. 51, pp. 107–115). North-Holland.

Drew, R., Smith, W., Roche, T., Blackwell, S., Gray, S., Iannucci, A., & Martin, I. (2009). *The Thick Of It*, episode 3.5. Director: Armando Iannucci.

Du, X., Qin, Y., Tu, S., Yin, H., Wang, T., Yu, C., & Qiu, J. (2013). Differentiation of stages in joke comprehension: Evidence from an ERP study. *International Journal of Psychology*, 48(2), 149–157.

Dunbar, R. I. M., Baron, R., Frangou, A., Pearce, E., Van Leeuwen, E. J., Stow, J., . . . Van Vugt, M. (2012). Social laughter is correlated with an elevated pain threshold. *Proceedings of the Royal Society B: Biological Sciences*, 279(1731), 1161–1167.

Dunbar, R. I. M., Launay, J., & Curry, O. (2016). The complexity of jokes is limited by cognitive constraints on mentalizing. *Human Nature*, 27(2), 130–140.

Dunbar, R. I. M., Marriott, A., & Duncan, N. D. (1997). Human conversational behavior. *Human Nature*, 8(3), 231–246.

Dyck, K. T., & Holtzman, S. (2013). Understanding humor styles and well-being: The importance of social relationships and gender. *Personality and Individual Differences*, 55(1), 53–58.

Edwards, K. R., & Martin, R. A. (2012). Do humorous people take poorer care of their health? Associations between humor styles and substance use. *Europe's Journal of Psychology*, 8(4).

Eisend, M. (2009). A meta-analysis of humor in advertising. *Journal of the Academy of Marketing Science, 37*(2), 191–203.

Eisend, M. (2011). How humor in advertising works: A meta-analytic test of alternative models. *Marketing Letters, 22*(2), 115–132.

Eisend, M. (2018). Explaining the use and effects of humour in advertising: An evolutionary perspective. *International Journal of Advertising, 37*(4), 526–547.

Engelthaler, T., & Hills, T. T. (2018). Humor norms for 4,997 English words. *Behavior Research Methods, 50*(3), 1116–1124.

Evans, J. B., Slaughter, J. E., Ellis, A. P., & Rivin, J. M. (2019). Gender and the evaluation of humor at work. *Journal of Applied Psychology, 104*(8), 1077.

Eysenck, H. J. (1942). The appreciation of humour: An experimental and theoretical study 1. *British Journal of Psychology. General Section, 32*(4), 295–309.

Falanga, R., De Caroli, M. E., & Sagone, E. (2014). Humor styles, self-efficacy and prosocial tendencies in middle adolescents. *Procedia-Social and Behavioral Sciences, 127*, 214–218.

Feingold, A. (1992). Gender differences in mate selection preferences: A test of the parental investment model. *Psychological Bulletin, 112*(1), 125.

Feng, Y. J., Chan, Y. C., & Chen, H. C. (2014). Specialization of neural mechanisms underlying the three-stage model in humor processing: An ERP study. *Journal of Neurolinguistics, 32*, 59–70.

Fere M. C. (1903). Le fou rire prodromique. *Revue Neurologique, 11*, 353–358.

Fisher, S., & Fisher, R. L. (1981). *Pretend the world is funny and forever: A psychological analysis of comedians, clowns, and actors.* London: Psychology Press.

Fitts, S. D., Sebby, R. A., & Zlokovich, M. S. (2009). Humor styles as mediators of the shyness-loneliness relationship. *North American Journal of Psychology, 11*(2).

Foote, R., & Woodward, J. (1973). A preliminary investigation of obscene language. *The Journal of Psychology, 83*(2), 263–275.

Ford, T. E. (1997). Effects of stereotypical television portrayals of African-Americans on person perception. *Social Psychology Quarterly*, 266–275.

Ford, T. E. (2000). Effects of sexist humor on tolerance of sexist events. *Personality and Social Psychology Bulletin, 26*(9), 1094–1107.

Ford, T. E., Boxer, C. F., Armstrong, J., & Edel, J. R. (2008). More than "just a joke": The prejudice-releasing function of sexist humor. *Personality and Social Psychology Bulletin, 34*(2), 159–170.

Ford, T. E., Lappi, S. K., & Holden, C. J. (2016). Personality, humor styles and happiness: Happy people have positive humor styles. *Europe's Journal of Psychology, 12*(3), 320.

Ford, T. E., McCreight, K. A., & Richardson, K. (2014). Affective style, humor styles and happiness. *Europe's Journal of Psychology, 10*(3), 451–463.

Ford, T. E., Richardson, K., & Petit, W. E. (2015). Disparagement humor and prejudice: Contemporary theory and research. *Humor, 28*(2), 171–186.

Ford, T. E., Wentzel, E. R., & Lorion, J. (2001). Effects of exposure to sexist humor on perceptions of normative tolerance of sexism. *European Journal of Social Psychology, 31*(6), 677–691.

Foster, J. A., & Reid, J. (1983). Humor and its relationship to students' assessments of the counsellor. *Canadian Journal of Counselling and Psychotherapy, 17*(3).

Fraley, B., & Aron, A. (2004). The effect of a shared humorous experience on closeness in initial encounters. *Personal Relationships, 11*(1), 61–78.

Freud, S. (1960). *Jokes and their relation to the unconscious* (James Strachey, Trans.). New York: Routledge.

Fridlund, A. J., & Loftis, J. M. (1990). Relations between tickling and humorous laughter: Preliminary support for the Darwin-Hecker hypothesis. *Biological Psychology, 30*(2), 141–150.

Fridlund, A. J., Sabini, J. P., Hedlund, L. E., Schaut, J. A., Shenker, J. I., & Knauer, M. J. (1990). Audience effects on solitary faces during imagery: Displaying to the people in your head. *Journal of Nonverbal Behavior, 14*(2), 113–137.

Fritz, H. L. (2020, in press). Why are humor styles associated with well-being, and does social competence matter? Examining relations to psychological and physical well-being, reappraisal, and social support. *Personality and Individual Differences, 154*, 109641.

Fritz, H. L., Russek, L. N., & Dillon, M. M. (2017). Humor use moderates the relation of stressful life events with psychological distress. *Personality and Social Psychology Bulletin, 43*(6), 845–859.

Fry Jr, W. F. (1987). Humor and paradox. *American Behavioral Scientist, 30*(3), 42–71.

Fry Jr, W. F., & Salameh, W. A. (1987). *Handbook of humor and psychotherapy: Advances in the clinical use of humor.* New York: Professional Resource Exchange, Inc.

Fry, W. F., & Savin, W. M. (1988). Mirthful laughter and blood pressure. *Humor, 1*(1), 49–62.

Frymier, A. B., Wanzer, M. B., & Wojtaszczyk, A. M. (2008). Assessing students' perceptions of inappropriate and appropriate teacher humor. *Communication Education, 57*(2), 266–288.

Fuller, R. G., & Sheehy-Skeffington, A. (1974). Effects of group laughter on responses to humourous material, a replication and extension. *Psychological Reports*, 35(1), 531–534.

Gallahorn, G. E. (1971). The use of taboo words by psychiatric ward personnel. *Psychiatry*, 34(3), 309–321.

Gallois, C., & Callan, V. J. (1985). Situational influences on perceptions of accented speech. In J Forgas (Ed.), *Language and social situations* (pp. 159–173). New York: Springer.

Gallup Jr, G. G., Ampel, B. C., Wedberg, N., & Pogosjan, A. (2014). Do orgasms give women feedback about mate choice?. *Evolutionary Psychology*, 12(5), 147470491401200507.

Gardner, H., Albert, M. L., & Weintraub, S. (1975). Comprehending a word: The influence of speed and redundancy on auditory comprehension in aphasia. *Cortex*, 11(2), 155–162.

Gest, S. D., Sesma, A., Masten, A. S., & Tellegen, A. (2006). Childhood peer reputation as a predictor of competence and symptoms 10 years later. *Journal of Abnormal Child Psychology*, 34(4), 507.

Goel, V., & Dolan, R. J. (2001). The functional anatomy of humor: Segregating cognitive and affective components. *Nature Neuroscience*, 4(3), 237–238.

Greengross, G. (2013). Humor and aging-a mini-review. *Gerontology*, 59(5), 448–453.

Greengross, G., & Miller, G. F. (2009). The Big Five personality traits of professional comedians compared to amateur comedians, comedy writers, and college students. *Personality and Individual Differences*, 47(2), 79–83.

Greengross, G., & Miller, G. F. (2011). Humor ability reveals intelligence, predicts mating success, and is higher in males. *Intelligence*, 39(4), 188–192.

Greengross, G., Silvia, P. J., & Nusbaum, E. C. (2020). Sex differences in humor production ability: A meta-analysis. *Journal of Research in Personality*, 84, 103886.

Greenwood, D. (2010). Of sad men and dark comedies: Mood and gender effects on entertainment media preferences. *Mass Communication and Society*, 13(3), 232–249.

Greenwood, D., & Isbell, L. M. (2002). Ambivalent sexism and the dumb blonde: Men's and women's reactions to sexist jokes. *Psychology of Women Quarterly*, 26(4), 341–350.

Greig, J. Y. T. (1923). *The psychology of laughter and comedy*. London: Allen & Unwin.

Gruner, C. R. (1976). Wit and humor in mass communication. In A. J. Chapman & H. C. Foot (Eds.), *Humor and laughter: Theory, research, and applications* (pp. 287–311). Transaction Publishers.

Guenter, H., Schreurs, B., Van Emmerik, I. H., Gijsbers, W., & Van Iterson, A. (2013). How adaptive and maladaptive humor influence well-being at work: A diary study. *Humor, 26*(4), 573–594.

Gulas, C. S., Larsen, J. E., & Coleman, J. W. (2009). Brand and message recall: The effects of situational involvement and brand symbols in the marketing of real estate services. *Services Marketing Quarterly, 30*(4), 333–341.

Gulas, C. S., McKeage, K. K., & Weinberger, M. G. (2010). It's just a joke. *Journal of Advertising, 39*(4), 109–120.

Hahn, C. M., & Campbell, L. J. (2016). Birds of a feather laugh together: An investigation of humour style similarity in married couples. *Europe's Journal of Psychology, 12*(3), 406.

Hall, G. S., & Allin, A. (1897). The psychology of tickling, laughing, and the comic. *The American Journal of Psychology, 9*(1), 1–41.

Hall, J. A. (2017). Humor in romantic relationships: A meta-analysis. *Personal Relationships, 24*(2), 306–322.

Hall, J. A. (2019). Humor production in long-term romantic relationships: What the lack of moderation by sex reveals about humor's role in mating. *Humor, 32*(3), 343–359.

Harris, R. J., Hoekstra, S. J., Scott, C. L., Sanborn, F. W., Karafa, J. A., & Brandenburg, J. D. (2000). Young men's and women's different autobiographical memories of the experience of seeing frightening movies on a date. *Media Psychology, 2*(3), 245–268.

Harrison, L. K., Carroll, D., Burns, V. E., Corkill, A. R., Harrison, C. M., Ring, C., & Drayson, M. (2000). Cardiovascular and secretory immunoglobulin A reactions to humorous, exciting, and didactic film presentations. *Biological Psychology, 52*(2), 113–126.

Hehl, F. J., & Ruch, W. (1985). The location of sense of humor within comprehensive personality spaces: An exploratory study. *Personality and Individual Differences, 6*(6), 703–715.

Heintz, S. (2017). Putting a spotlight on daily humor behaviors: Dimensionality and relationships with personality, subjective well-being, and humor styles. *Personality and Individual Differences, 104*, 407–412.

Heintz, S., & Ruch, W. (2019). From four to nine styles: An update on individual differences in humor. *Personality and Individual Differences, 141*, 7–12.

Hendriks, H., & Janssen, L. (2018). Frightfully funny: Combining threat and humour in health messages for men and women. *Psychology & Health, 33*(5), 594–613.

Henkin, B., & Fish, J. M. (1986). Gender and personality differences in the appreciation of cartoon humor. *The Journal of Psychology*, 120(2), 157–175.

Hiranandani, N. A., & Yue, X. D. (2014). Humour styles, gelotophobia and self-esteem among C hinese and I ndian university students. *Asian Journal of Social Psychology*, 17(4), 319–324.

Hodson, G., MacInnis, C. C., & Rush, J. (2010). Prejudice-relevant correlates of humor temperaments and humor styles. *Personality and Individual Differences*, 49(5), 546–549.

Hone, L. S., Hurwitz, W., & Lieberman, D. (2015). Sex differences in preferences for humor: A replication, modification, and extension. *Evolutionary Psychology*, 13(1), 147470491501300110.

Hooper, J., Sharpe, D., & Roberts, S. G. B. (2016). Are men funnier than women, or do we just think they are?. *Translational Issues in Psychological Science*, 2(1), 54.

Houser, M. L., Cowan, R. L., & West, D. A. (2007). Investigating a new education frontier: Instructor communication behavior in CD-ROM; Do traditionally positive behaviors translate into this new environment? *Communication Quarterly*, 55(1), 19–38.

Howrigan, D. P., & MacDonald, K. B. (2008). Humor as a mental fitness indicator. *Evolutionary Psychology*, 6(4), 625–666

Hughes, G. (1998). *Swearing: A social history of foul language, oaths and profanity in English*. London: Penguin UK.

Jay, T. (1980). Sex roles and dirty word usage: A review of the literature and a reply to Haas. *Psychological Bulletin*, 88(3), 614–621.

Jay, T. (2009). The utility and ubiquity of taboo words. *Perspectives on Psychological Science*, 4(2), 153–161.

Jiang, F., Yue, X. D., & Lu, S. (2011). Different attitudes toward humor between Chinese and American students: Evidence from the Implicit Association Test. *Psychological Reports*, 109(1), 99–107.

Kaplan, R. M., & Pascoe, G. C. (1977). Humorous lectures and humorous examples: Some effects upon comprehension and retention. *Journal of Educational Psychology*, 69(1), 61.

Kataoka, S., Hori, A., Shirakawa, T., & Hirose, G. (1997). Paramedian pontine infarction: Neurological/topographical correlation. *Stroke*, 28(4), 809–815.

Kazarian, S. S., & Martin, R. A. (2004). Humour styles, personality, and well-being among Lebanese university students. *European journal of Personality*, 18(3), 209–219.

Kelly, J. P., & Solomon, P. J. (1975). Humor in television advertising. *Journal of Advertising*, 4(3), 31–35.

Kennison, S. M., & Messer, R. H. (2017). Cursing as a form of risk-taking. *Current Psychology*, 36(1), 119–126.

Kerkkanen, P., Kuiper, N. A., & Martin, R. A. (2004). Sense of humor, physical health, and well-being at work: A three-year longitudinal study of Finnish police officers. *Humor*, 17(1/2), 21–36.

Killinger, B. (1987). Humor in psychotherapy: A shift to a new perspective. In *Handbook of humor and psychotherapy: Advances in the clinical use of humor* (pp. 21–40). New York: Professional Resource Exchange, Inc.

Kirkegaard, E. O. (2017). Sex distribution, life expectancy and educational attainment of comedians. *Mankind Quarterly*, 58(1), 180–194.

Klerk, V. D. (1991). Expletives: Men only? *Communications Monographs*, 58(2), 156–169.

Koestler, A. (1964). *The act of creation*. London: Macmillan.

Kohler, K. J. (2008). 'Speech-smile','speech-laugh','laughter' and their sequencing in dialogic interaction. *Phonetica*, 65(1–2), 1–18.

Korb, S., Grandjean, D., Samson, A. C., Delplanque, S., & Scherer, K. R. (2012). Stop laughing! Humor perception with and without expressive suppression. *Social Neuroscience*, 7(5), 510–524.

Krems, J. A., & Dunbar, R. I. (2013). Clique size and network characteristics in hyperlink cinema. *Human Nature*, 24(4), 414–429.

Krys, K., Vauclair, C. M., Capaldi, C. A., Lun, V. M. C., Bond, M. H., Domínguez-Espinosa, A., . . . Antalíková, R. (2016). Be careful where you smile: Culture shapes judgments of intelligence and honesty of smiling individuals. *Journal of Nonverbal Behavior*, 40(2), 101–116.

Kubie, L. S. (1970). The destructive potential of humor in psychotherapy.In W. M. Mendel (Ed.), *A Celebration of Laughter* (pp. 67–81). Los Angeles: Mara Books.

Kubie, L. S. (1971).The destructive potential of humor in psychotherapy. *American Journal of Psychiatry*, 127(7), 861–866.

Kuiper, N. A., & Nicholl, S. (2004). Thoughts of feeling better? Sense of humor and physical health. *Humor*, 17(1–2), 37–66.

Kunkel, D., Wilson, B., Donnerstein, E., Linz, D., Smith, S., Gray, T., . . . Potter, W. J. (1995). Standpoint: Measuring television violence: The importance of context. *Journal of Broadcasting & Electronic Media*, 39(2), 284–291.

Labott, S. M., Ahleman, S., Wolever, M. E., & Martin, R. B. (1990). The physiological and psychological effects of the expression and inhibition of emotion. *Behavioral Medicine*, 16(4), 182–189.

La Fave, L. (1972). Humor judgments as a function of reference groups and identification classes. In J. H. Goldstein & P. McGhee (Eds.), *The psychology of humor: Theoretical perspectives and empirical issues* (pp. 195–210). Amsterdam: Elsevier.

La Fave, L., Haddad, J., & Maesen, W. A. (1976). Superiority, enhanced self-esteem, and perceived incongruity humour theory. In A. J. Chapman & H. C. Foot (Eds.), *Humor and laughter: Theory, research and applications* (pp. 63, 91). New York: Transaction Publishers.

LaFrance, M., Hecht, M. A., & Paluck, E. L. (2003). The contingent smile: A meta-analysis of sex differences in smiling. *Psychological Bulletin*, 129(2), 305.

Laroche, M., Nepomuceno, M. V., Huang, L., & Richard, M. O. (2011). What's so funny?: The use of humor in magazine advertising in the United States, China, and France. *Journal of Advertising Research*, 51(2), 404–416.

Laskowski, K., & Burger, S. (2007). On the correlation between perceptual and contextual aspects of laughter in meetings. *Proc. ICPhSWS on Phonetics of Laughter*, 55–60.

Lefcourt, H. M., Davidson-Katz, K., & Kueneman, K. (1990). Humor and immune-system functioning. *Humor*, 3(3), 305–322.

Lefcourt, H. M., Davidson-Katz, K., Prkachin, K. M., & Mills, D. E. (1997). Humor as a stress moderator in the prediction of blood pressure obtained during five stressful tasks. *Journal of Research in Personality*, 31(4), 523–542.

Leonidas, H., Christina, B., & Yorgos, Z. (2009). The effects of culture and product type on the use of humor in Greek tv advertising: An application of speck's humorous message taxonomy. *Journal of Current Issues & Research in Advertising*, 31(1), 43–61.

Lepori, G. M. (2015). Positive mood and investment decisions: Evidence from comedy movie attendance in the US. *Research in International Business and Finance*, 34, 142–163.

Leventhal, H., & Cupchik, G. C. (1975). The informational and facilitative effects of an audience upon expression and the evaluation of humorous stimuli. *Journal of Experimental Social Psychology*, 11(4), 363–380.

Leventhal, H., & Mace, W. (1970). The effect of laughter on evaluation of a slapstick movie 1. *Journal of Personality*, 38(1), 16–30.

Levine, J. B. (1976). The feminine routine. *Journal of Communication*, 26, 173–175.

Li, N. P., Griskevicius, V., Durante, K. M., Jonason, P. K., Pasisz, D. J., & Aumer, K. (2009). An evolutionary perspective on humor: Sexual selection or interest indication?. *Personality and Social Psychology Bulletin*, 35(7), 923–936.

Lin, C. H., Yen, H. R., & Chuang, S. C. (2006). The effects of emotion and need for cognition on consumer choice involving risk. *Marketing Letters*, 17(1), 47–60.

Lockard, J. S., Fahrenbruch, C. E., Smith, J. L., & Morgan, C. J. (1977). Smiling and laughter: Different phyletic origins?. *Bulletin of the Psychonomic Society*, 10(3), 183–186.

Long, D. L., & Graesser, A. C. (1988). Wit and humor in discourse processing. *Discourse Processes*, 11(1), 35–60.

Love, A. M., & Deckers, L. H. (1989). Humor appreciation as a function of sexual, aggressive, and sexist content. *Sex Roles*, 20(11–12), 649–654.

Lu, J. G., Martin, A. E., Usova, A., & Galinsky, A. D. (2019). Creativity and humor across cultures: Where Aha meets Haha. In S. R. Luria, J. Baer, & J. C. Kaufman (Eds.), *Creativity and humor* (pp. 183–203). New York: Academic Press.

Machlev, M., & Karlin, N. J. (2017). The relationship between instructor use of different types of humor and student interest in course material. *College Teaching*, 65(4), 192–200.

Madden, T. J., & Weinberger, M. G. (1982). The effects of humor on attention in magazine advertising. *Journal of Advertising*, 11(3), 8–14.

Maio, G. R., Olson, J. M., & Bush, J. E. (1997). Telling jokes that disparage social groups: Effects on the joke teller's stereotypes 1. *Journal of Applied Social Psychology*, 27(22), 1986–2000.

Mak, W., & Carpenter, B. D. (2007). Humor comprehension in older adults. *Journal of the International Neuropsychological Society*, 13(4), 606.

Marci, C. D., Moran, E. K., & Orr, S. P. (2004). Physiologic evidence for the interpersonal role of laughter during psychotherapy. *The Journal of Nervous and Mental Disease*, 192(10), 689–695.

Marinkovic, K., Baldwin, S., Courtney, M. G., Witzel, T., Dale, A. M., & Halgren, E. (2011). Right hemisphere has the last laugh: Neural dynamics of joke appreciation. *Cognitive, Affective, & Behavioral Neuroscience*, 11(1), 113–130.

Martin, G. N. (2019). (Why) do you like scary movies? A systematic review of the psychology of horror cinema. *Frontiers in Psychology*. Retrieved from www.frontiersin.org/articles/10.3389/fpsyg.2019.02298/full

Martin, G. N., & Carlson, N. R. (2018). *Psychology* (6th ed.). Harlow: Pearson Education.

Martin, G. N., & Gray, C. D. (1996). The effects of audience laughter on retrospective and spontaneous response to humour. *Journal of Social Psychology, 136*(2), 221–231.

Martin, G. N., Sadler, S. Barrett, C., & Bevan, A. (2008). Measuring responses to humor: How the testing context affects individuals' reaction to comedy. *Humor: The International Journal of Humor Studies, 21*(2), 143–155.

Martin, G. N., & Sullivan, E. (2013). Cross-cultural differences in sense of humour: A comparison between British, Australian and American respondents, *North American Journal of Psychology, 15*, 375–384.

Martin, J., Rychlowska, M., Wood, A., & Niedenthal, P. (2017). Smiles as multipurpose social signals. *Trends in Cognitive Sciences, 21*(11), 864–877.

Martin, R. A. (2006). *The psychology of humor: An integrative approach*. New York: Elsevier.

Martin, R. A., & Ford, T. (2018). *The psychology of humor: An integrative approach*. New York: Academic Press.

Martin, R. A., & Kuiper, N. A. (1999). Daily occurrence of laughter: Relationships with age, gender, and Type A personality. *Humor, 12*, 355–384.

Martin, R. A., & Lefcourt, H. M. (1983). Sense of humor as a moderator of the relation between stressors and moods. *Journal of Personality and Social Psychology, 45*(6), 1313.

Martin, R. A., & Lefcourt, H. M. (1984). Situational humor response questionnaire: Quantitative measure of sense of humor. *Journal of Personality and Social Psychology, 47*(1), 145.

Martin, R. A., Puhlik-Doris, P., Larsen, G., Gray, J., & Weir, K. (2003). Individual differences in uses of humor and their relation to psychological well-being: Development of the Humor Styles Questionnaire. *Journal of Research in Personality, 37*(1), 48–75.

McDougall, W. (1903). The theory of laughter. *Nature, 67*(1736), 318–319.

McGee, E., & Shevlin, M. (2009). Effect of humor on interpersonal attraction and mate selection. *The Journal of Psychology, 143*(1), 67–77.

McGhee, P. E. (1979). *Humor, its origin and development*. New York: WH Freeman.

McIntosh, W. D., Murray, J. D., Murray, R. M., & Manian, S. (2003). What's so funny about a poke in the eye? The prevalence of violence in comedy films and its relation to social and economic threat in the United States, 1951–2000. *Mass Communication and Society*, 6(4), 345–360.

Meeus, W., & Mahieu, P. (2009). You can see the funny side, can't you? Pupil humour with the teacher as target. *Educational Studies*, 35(5), 553–560.

Meletti, S., Cantalupo, G., Benuzzi, F., Mai, R., Tassi, L., Gasparini, E., . . . Nichelli, P. (2012). Fear and happiness in the eyes: An intra-cerebral event-related potential study from the human amygdala. *Neuropsychologia*, 50(1), 44–54.

Melville, H (1852). *Pierre; or, The Ambiguities*. Harper & Brothers: New York.

Mendiburo-Seguel, A., Páez, D., & Martínez-Sánchez, F. (2015). Humor styles and personality: A meta-analysis of the relation between humor styles and the Big Five personality traits. *Scandinavian Journal of Psychology*, 56(3), 335–340.

Menezes, C., & Igarashi, Y. (2006). The speech laugh spectrum. *Proceedings of the Speech Production, Brazil*, 157–164.

Mickes, L., Walker, D. E., Parris, J. L., Mankoff, R., & Christenfeld, N. J. (2012). Who's funny: Gender stereotypes, humor production, and memory bias. *Psychonomic Bulletin & Review*, 19(1), 108–112.

Miller, G. F. (2000). Mental traits as fitness indicators: Expanding evolutionary psychology's adaptationism. *Annals of the New York Academy Of Sciences*, 907, 62–74.

Miller, G. F. (2007). Sexual selection for moral virtues. *The Quarterly Review of Biology*, 82(2), 97–125.

Mittal, V. K., & Yegnanarayana, B. (2015). Analysis of production characteristics of laughter. *Computer Speech & Language*, 30(1), 99–115.

Mobbs, D., Greicius, M. D., Abdel-Azim, E., Menon, V., & Reiss, A. L. (2003). Humor modulates the mesolimbic reward centers. *Neuron*, 40(5), 1041–1048.

Moore, T. E., Griffiths, K., & Payne, B. (1987). Gender, attitudes towards women, and the appreciation of sexist humor. *Sex Roles*, 16(9–10), 521–531.

Mora-Ripoll, R. (2011). Potential health benefits of simulated laughter: A narrative review of the literature and recommendations for future research. *Complementary Therapies in Medicine*, 19(3), 170–177.

Moran, J. M., Wig, G. S., Adams Jr, R. B., Janata, P., & Kelley, W. M. (2004). Neural correlates of humor detection and appreciation. *Neuroimage*, 21(3), 1055–1060.

Morreall, J. (1986). *The philosophy of laughter and humor*. New York: SUNY Press.

Moyer-Gusé, E., Mahood, C., & Brookes, S. (2011). Entertainment-education in the context of humor: Effects on safer sex intentions and risk perceptions. *Health Communication*, 26(8), 765–774.

Muris, P., Merckelbach, H., Otgaar, H., & Meijer, E. (2017). The malevolent side of human nature: A meta-analysis and critical review of the literature on the dark triad (narcissism, Machiavellianism, and psychopathy). *Perspectives on Psychological Science*, 12(2), 183–204.

Myers, S. A., Ropog, B. L., & Rodgers, R. P. (1997). Sex differences in humor. *Psychological Reports*, 81(1), 221–222.

Nakamura, T., Matsui, T., Utsumi, A., Yamazaki, M., Makita, K., Harada, T., . . . Sadato, N. (2018). The role of the amygdala in incongruity resolution: The case of humor comprehension. *Social Neuroscience*, 13(5), 553–565.

Nevo, O., Nevo, B., & Yin, J. L. S. (2001). Singaporean humor: A cross-cultural, cross-gender comparison. *The Journal of General Psychology*, 128(2), 143–156.

Nezu, A. M., Nezu, C. M., & Blissett, S. E. (1988). Sense of humor as a moderator of the relation between stressful events and psychological distress: A prospective analysis. *Journal of Personality and Social Psychology*, 54(3), 520.

Nosanchuk, T. A., & Lightstone, J. (1974). Canned laughter and public and private conformity. *Journal of Personality and Social Psychology*, 29(1), 153.

Olson, J. M., Maio, G. R., & Hobden, K. L. (1999). The (null) effects of exposure to disparagement humor on stereotypes and attitudes. *Humor: International Journal of Humor Research*, 12(2), 195–219.

Olson, M. L., Hugelshofer, D. S., Kwon, P., & Reff, R. C. (2005). Rumination and dysphoria: The buffering role of adaptive forms of humor. *Personality and Individual Differences*, 39(8), 1419–1428.

Oppliger, P. A., & Shouse, E. (2020). *The Dark Side of Stand-Up Comedy*. Springer International Publishing.

Osaka, M., Yaoi, K., Minamoto, T., & Osaka, N. (2014). Serial changes of humor comprehension for four-frame comic Manga: An fMRI study. *Scientific Reports*, 4(1), 1–9.

Owren, M. J. (2007). Understanding acoustics and function in spontaneous human laughter. *The Phonetics of Laughter*, 1.

Owren, M. J., & Bachorowski, J. A. (2003). Reconsidering the evolution of non-linguistic communication: The case of laughter. *Journal of Nonverbal Behavior*, 27(3), 183–200.

Özdoğru, A. A., & McMorris, R. F. (2013). Humorous cartoons in college textbooks: Student perceptions and learning. Humor, 26(1), 135–154.

Paulhus, D. L., & Williams, K. M. (2002). The dark triad of personality: Narcissism, Machiavellianism, and psychopathy. Journal of Research in Personality, 36(6), 556–563.

Perlini, A. H., Nenonen, R. G., & Lind, D. L. (1999). Effects of humor on test anxiety and performance. Psychological Reports, 84(3 suppl), 1203–1213.

Peterson, J. P., & Pollio, H. R. (1982). Therapeutic effectiveness of differentially targeted humorous remarks in group psychotherapy. Group, 6(4), 39–50.

Pisanski, K., Cartei, V., McGettigan, C., Raine, J., & Reby, D. (2016). Voice modulation: A window into the origins of human vocal control?. Trends in Cognitive Sciences, 20(4), 304–318.

Plessen, C. Y., Franken, F. R., Ster, C., Schmid, R. R., Wolfmayr, C., Mayer, A. M., . . . Maierwieser, R. J. (2020). Humor styles and personality: A systematic review and meta-analysis on the relations between humor styles and the Big Five personality traits. Personality and Individual Differences, 154, 109676.

Poeck, K. (1969). Pathophysiology of emotional disorders associated with brain damage. Disorders of higher nervous activity. Handbook of Clinical Neurology. Amsterdam: North Holland Publishing Co, 343.

Pollio, H. R., & Edgerly, J. W. (1976). Comedians and comic style. In A. J. Chapman & H. C. Foot (Eds.), Humor and laughter: Theory, research, and applications (pp. 215–242). London: Transaction Publishers.

Pollio, H. R., Edgerly, J. W., & Jordan, R. (1972). The comedian's world: Some tentative mappings. Psychological Reports, 30(2), 387–391.

Porterfield, A. L. (1987). Does sense of humor moderate the impact of life stress on psychological and physical well-being? Journal of Research in Personality, 21(3), 306–317.

Powell, J. P., & Andresen, L. W. (1985). Humour and teaching in higher education. Studies in Higher Education, 10(1), 79–90.

Priest, R. F., & Swain, J. E. (2002). Humor and its implications for leadership effectiveness. Humor, 15(2), 169–189.

Priest, R. F., & Thein, M. T. (2003). Humor appreciation in marriage: Spousal similarity, assortative mating, and disaffection. Humor, 16(1), 63–78.

Provine, R. R. (2004). Laughing, tickling, and the evolution of speech and self. Current Directions in Psychological Science, 13(6), 215–218.

Proyer, R. T., & Ruch, W. (2010). Enjoying and fearing laughter: Personality characteristics of gelotophobes, gelotophiles, and katagelasticists. *Psychological Test and Assessment Modeling*, 52(2), 148–160.

Reysen, S. (2006). A new predictor of likeability: Laughter. *North American Journal of Psychology*, 8(2).

Rhodes, L. A. (1983). Laughter and suffering: Sinhalese interpretations of the use of ritual humor. *Social Science & Medicine*, 17(14), 979–984.

Robinson, D. T., & Smith-Lovin, L. (2001). Getting a laugh: Gender, status, and humor in task discussions. *Social Forces*, 80(1), 123–158.

Rodd, J. M., Gilbert, R. A., & Betts, H. N. (2017). The role of learning mechanisms in understanding spoken words. *Cognition*, 40, 1095–1108.

Roeckelein, J. E. (2002). *The psychology of humor: A reference guide and annotated bibliography*. New York: Greenwood Press/Greenwood Publishing Group.

Romundstad, S., Svebak, S., Holen, A., & Holmen, J. (2016). A 15-year follow-up study of sense of humor and causes of mortality: The Nord-Trøndelag Health Study. *Psychosomatic Medicine*, 78(3), 345–353.

Ross, E., & Hall, J. A. (in press). The traditional sexual script and humor in courtship. *HUMOR: International Journal of Humor Research*.

Rosenheim, E., & Golan, G. (1986). Patients' reactions to humorous interventions in psychotherapy. *American Journal of Psychotherapy*, 40(1), 110–124.

Rotton, J. (1992). Trait humor and longevity: Do comics have the last laugh? *Health Psychology*, 11(4), 262.

Ruben, M. A., Hall, J. A., & Schmid Mast, M. (2015). Smiling in a job interview: When less is more. *The Journal of Social Psychology*, 155(2), 107–126.

Ruch, W. (Ed.). (2010). *The sense of humor: Explorations of a personality characteristic* (Vol. 3). Germany: Walter de Gruyter.

Ruch, W., & Heintz, S. (2017). Experimentally manipulating items informs on the (limited) construct and criterion validity of the Humor Styles Questionnaire. *Frontiers in Psychology*, 8, 616.

Ruch, W., Heintz, S., Platt, T., Wagner, L., & Proyer, R. T. (2018). Broadening humor: Comic styles differentially tap into temperament, character, and ability. *Frontiers in Psychology*, 9, 6.

Ruch, W., Platt, T., & Hofmann, J. (2014). The character strengths of class clowns. *Frontiers in Psychology*, 5, 1075.

Ruch, W., Platt, T., Proyer, R. T., & Chen, H. C. (2019). Humor and laughter, playfulness and cheerfulness: Upsides and downsides to a life of lightness. *Frontiers in Psychology*, 10, 730.

Ruch, W., & Proyer, R. T. (2009a). Extending the study of gelotophobia: On gelotophiles and katagelasticists. *Humor, 22*(1–2), 183–212.

Ruch, W., & Proyer, R. T. (2009b). Who fears being laughed at? The location of gelotophobia in the Eysenckian PEN-model of personality. *Personality and Individual Differences, 46*(5–6), 627–630.

Ryan, K. M., & Kanjorski, J. (1998). The enjoyment of sexist humor, rape attitudes, and relationship aggression in college students. *Sex Roles, 38*(9–10), 743–756.

Rychlowska, M., Jack, R. E., Garrod, O. G., Schyns, P. G., Martin, J. D., & Niedenthal, P. M. (2017). Functional smiles: Tools for love, sympathy, and war. *Psychological Science, 28*(9), 1259–1270.

Rychlowska, M., Miyamoto, Y., Matsumoto, D., Hess, U., Gilboa-Schechtman, E., Kamble, S., . . . Niedenthal, P. M. (2015). Heterogeneity of long-history migration explains cultural differences in reports of emotional expressivity and the functions of smiles. *Proceedings of the National Academy of Sciences, 112*(19), E2429–E2436.

Sala, F., Krupat, E., & Roter, D. (2002). Satisfaction and the use of humor by physicians and patients. *Psychology and Health, 17*(3), 269–280.

Salameh, W. A. (1980). Personality of the comedian: the theory of tragi-comicreconciliation. Unpublished doctoral dissertation. University of Montreal. Montreal. Canada.

Salavera, C., Usán, P., & Jarie, L. (2020). Styles of humor and social skills in students. Gender differences. *Current Psychology, 39*(2), 571–580.

Sari, S. V. (2016). Was it just joke? Cyberbullying perpetrations and their styles of humor. *Computers in Human Behavior, 54*, 555–559.

Saroglou, V., Lacour, C., & Demeure, M. E. (2010). Bad humor, bad marriage: Humor styles in divorced and married couples. *Europe's Journal of Psychology, 6*(3), 94–121.

Scharrer, E., Bergstrom, A., Paradise, A., & Ren, Q. (2006). Laughing to keep from crying: Humor and aggression in television commercial content. *Journal of Broadcasting & Electronic Media, 50*(4), 615–634.

Schermer, J. A., Martin, R. A., Martin, N. G., Lynskey, M. T., Trull, T. J., & Vernon, P. A. (2015). Humor styles and borderline personality. *Personality and Individual Differences, 87*, 158–161.

Schneider, M., Voracek, M., & Tran, U. S. (2018). "A joke a day keeps the doctor away?" Meta-analytical evidence of differential associations of habitual humor styles with mental health. *Scandinavian Journal of Psychology*, 59(3), 289–300.

Schwarz, U., Hoffmann, S., & Hutter, K. (2015). Do men and women laugh about different types of humor? A comparison of satire, sentimental comedy, and comic wit in print ads. *Journal of Current Issues & Research in Advertising*, 36(1), 70–87.

Shammi, P., & Stuss, D. T. (1999). Humour appreciation: A role of the right frontal lobe. *Brain*, 122(4), 657–666.

Shammi, P., & Stuss, D. T. (2003). The effects of normal aging on humor appreciation. *Journal of the International Neuropsychological Society*, 9(6), 855–863.

Shibata, M., Terasawa, Y., & Umeda, S. (2014). Integration of cognitive and affective networks in humor comprehension. *Neuropsychologia*, 65, 137–145.

Shultz, T. R. (1972). The role of incongruity and resolution in children's appreciation of cartoon humor. *Journal of Experimental Child Psychology*, 13(3), 456–477.

Sidelinger, R. J., & Tatum, N. T. (2019). Instructor humor as a moderator of instructors' inappropriate conversations and instructional dissent. *College Teaching*, 67(2), 120–129.

Smith, R. E., Ascough, J. C., Ettinger, R. F., & Nelson, D. A. (1971). Humor, anxiety, and task performance. *Journal of Personality and Social Psychology*, 19(2), 243.

Smyth, M. M., & Fuller, R. G. (1972). Effects of group laughter on responses to humorous material. *Psychological Reports*, 30(1), 132–134.

Speck, P. S. (1991). The humorous message taxonomy: A framework for the study of humorous ads. *Current Issues and Research in Advertising*, 13(1–2), 1–44.

Spencer, H. (1860/1911), *On the Physiology of Laughter, Essays on Education, Etc.*, London: Dent.

Sroufe, L. A., & Wunsch, J. P. (1972). The development of laughter in the first year of life. *Child Development*, 1326–1344.

Stebbins, R.A. (1980), The role of humour in teaching: strategies and self-expression, In P. Woods, (Ed), *Teacher Strategies*, Croom Helm, London.

Stephens, R., & Robertson, O. (2020). Swearing as a response to pain: Assessing hypoalgesic effects of novel "swear" words. *Frontiers in Psychology*, 11, 723.

Sternthal, B., & Craig, C. S. (1973). Humor in advertising. *Journal of Marketing*, 37(4), 12–18.

Stewart, P. A. (2012). *Debatable humor: Laughing matters on the 2008 presidential primary campaign*. New York: Lexington Books.

Stewart, P. A., Eubanks, A. D., Dye, R. G., Gong, Z. H., Bucy, E. P., Wicks, R. H., & Eidelman, S. (2018). Candidate performance and observable audience response: Laughter and applause–Cheering during the first 2016 Clinton–Trump presidential debate. *Frontiers in Psychology*, 9, 1182.

Stewart, S., & Thompson, D. R. (2015). Does comedy kill? A retrospective, longitudinal cohort, nested case–control study of humour and longevity in 53 British comedians. *International Journal of Cardiology*, 180, 258–261.

Stewart, S., Wiley, J. F., McDermott, C. J., & Thompson, D. R. (2016). Is the last "man" standing in comedy the least funny? A retrospective cohort study of elite stand-up comedians versus other entertainers. *International Journal of Cardiology*, 220, 789–793.

Strack, F., Martin, L. L., & Stepper, S. (1988). Inhibiting and facilitating conditions of the human smile: A nonobtrusive test of the facial feedback hypothesis. *Journal of Personality and Social Psychology*, 54(5), 768.

Suls, J. M. (1977). Cognitive and disparagement theories of humor: A theoretical and empirical synthesis. In A. J. Chapman & H. C. Foot (Eds.), *Humor and laughter: Theory, research, and applications* (pp. 287–311). London: Transaction Publishers.

Svebak, S. (1996). The development of the sense of humor questionnaire: From SHQ to SHQ-6. *Humor*, 9(3–4), 341–362.

Szameitat, D. P., Alter, K., Szameitat, A. J., Wildgruber, D., Sterr, A., & Darwin, C. J. (2009). Acoustic profiles of distinct emotional expressions in laughter. *The Journal of the Acoustical Society of America*, 126(1), 354–366.

Szameitat, D. P., Kreifelts, B., Alter, K., Szameitat, A. J., Sterr, A., Grodd, W., & Wildgruber, D. (2010). It is not always tickling: Distinct cerebral responses during perception of different laughter types. *Neuroimage*, 53(4), 1264–1271.

Szymaniak, K., & Kałowski, P. (2020). Trait anger and sarcasm use. *Personality and Individual Differences*, 154, 109662.

Tanaka, H., & Campbell, N. (2011, August). Acoustic features of four types of laughter in natural conversational speech. Hong Kong: ICPhS XVII (pp. 1958–1961).

Tanaka, H., & Campbell, N. (2014). Classification of social laughter in natural conversational speech. *Computer Speech & Language*, 28(1), 314–325.

Tanaka, M., & Sumitsuji, N. (1991). Electromyographic study of facial expressions during pathological laughing and crying. *Electromyography and Clinical Neurophysiology*, 31(7), 399.

Thomas, C. A., & Esses, V. M. (2004). Individual differences in reactions to sexist humor. *Group Processes & Intergroup Relations*, 7(1), 89–100.

Thorson, J. A., & Powell, F. C. (1993). Development and validation of a multidimensional sense of humor scale. *Journal of Clinical Psychology*, 49(1), 13–23.

Tsai, M. N., Wu, C. L., Chang, Y. L., & Chen, H. C. (2019). Humor styles in marriage: How similar are husband and wife?. *Psychological Reports*, 122(6), 2331–2347.

Tsukawaki, R., & Imura, T. (2019). Preliminary verification of instructional humor processing theory: Mediators between instructor humor and student learning. *Psychological Reports*. doi:10.1177/0033294119868799

Tsukiura, T., & Cabeza, R. (2008). Orbitofrontal and hippocampal contributions to memory for face–name associations: The rewarding power of a smile. *Neuropsychologia*, 46(9), 2310–2319.

Tucker, R. P., Judah, M. R., O'Keefe, V. M., Mills, A. C., Lechner, W. V., Davidson, C. L., . . . Wingate, L. R. (2013). Humor styles impact the relationship between symptoms of social anxiety and depression. *Personality and Individual Differences*, 55(7), 823–827.

Uekermann, J., Channon, S., & Daum, I. (2006). Humor processing, mentalizing, and executive function in normal aging. *Journal of the International Neuropsychological Society*, 12(2), 184.

van der Wal, C. N., & Kok, R. N. (2019). Laughter-inducing therapies: Systematic review and meta-analysis. *Social Science & Medicine*, 232, 473–488.

Van Lancker, D., & Cummings, J. L. (1999). Expletives: Neurolinguistic and neurobehavioral perspectives on swearing. *Brain Research Reviews*, 31(1), 83–104.

Ventis, W. L., Higbee, G., & Murdock, S. A. (2001). Using humor in systematic desensitization to reduce fear. *The Journal of General Psychology*, 128(2), 241–253.

Veselka, L., Schermer, J. A., Martin, R. A., & Vernon, P. A. (2010). Relations between humor styles and the Dark Triad traits of personality. *Personality and Individual Differences*, 48(6), 772–774.

Vettin, J., & Todt, D. (2004). Laughter in conversation: Features of occurrence and acoustic structure. *Journal of Nonverbal Behavior*, 28(2), 93–115.

Vlahovic, T. A., Roberts, S., & Dunbar, R. (2012). Effects of duration and laughter on subjective happiness within different modes of communication. *Journal of Computer-Mediated Communication*, 17(4), 436–450.

Vrabel, J. K., Zeigler-Hill, V., & Shango, R. G. (2017). Spitefulness and humor styles. *Personality and Individual Differences*, 105, 238–243.

Wade, T. J., & Feldman, A. (2016). Sex and the perceived effectiveness of flirtation techniques. *Human Ethology Bulletin*, 30.

Wagenmakers, E. J., Beek, T., Dijkhoff, L., Gronau, Q. F., Acosta, A., Adams Jr, R. B., . . . Bulnes, L. C. (2016). Registered replication report: Strack, martin, & stepper (1988). *Perspectives on Psychological Science*, 11(6), 917–928.

Wagner, L. (2019). The social life of class clowns: Class clown behavior is associated with more friends, but also more aggressive behavior in the classroom. *Frontiers in Psychology*, 10, 604.

Walsh, D. G., & Hewitt, J. (1985). Giving men the come-on: Effect of eye contact and smiling in a bar environment. *Perceptual and Motor Skills*, 61(3), 873–874.

Wanzer, M. B., Frymier, A. B., & Irwin, J. (2010). An explanation of the relationship between instructor humor and student learning: Instructional humor processing theory. *Communication Education*, 59(1), 1–18.

Warren, C., & McGraw, A. P. (2016). When does humorous marketing hurt brands? *Journal of Marketing Behavior*, 2(1), 39–67.

Watson, K. K., Matthews, B. J., & Allman, J. M. (2007). Brain activation during sight gags and language-dependent humor. *Cerebral Cortex*, 17(2), 314–324.

Wattendorf, E., Westermann, B., Fiedler, K., Ritz, S., Redmann, A., Pfannmöller, J., . . . Celio, M. R. (2019). Laughter is in the air: Involvement of key nodes of the emotional motor system in the anticipation of tickling. *Social Cognitive and Affective Neuroscience*, 14(8), 837–847.

Weisfeld, G. E., Nowak, N. T., Lucas, T., Weisfeld, C. C., Imamoğlu, E. O., Butovskaya, M., . . . Parkhill, M. R. (2011). Do women seek humorousness in men because it signals intelligence? A cross-cultural test. *Humor*, 24(4), 435–462.

Welsford, E. (1935). *The Fool: His Social and Literary History*. London: Faber and Faber.

Welsford, E. (1961). *The fool: His social and literary history*. New York: Doubleday.

West, M. S., & Martin, M. M. (2019). Students' perceptions of instructor appropriateness and humor homophily. *Communication Education*, 68(3), 328–349.

Wicker, F. W., Thorelli, I. M., Barron III, W. L., & Ponder, M. R. (1981). Relationships among affective and cognitive factors in humor. *Journal of Research in Personality*, 15(3), 359–370.

Wild, B., Rodden, F. A., Grodd, W., & Ruch, W. (2003). Neural correlates of laughter and humour. *Brain*, 126(10), 2121–2138.

Wildgruber, D., Szameitat, D. P., Ethofer, T., Brueck, C., Alter, K., Grodd, W., & Kreifelts, B. (2013). Different types of laughter modulate connectivity within distinct parts of the laughter perception network. *PloS One*, 8(5), e63441.

Wilson, S. A. K. (1924).Pathological laughing and crying. *Journal of Neurology and Psychopathology*, 4, 299–333.

Woltman Elpers, J. L., Mukherjee, A., & Hoyer, W. D. (2004). Humor in television advertising: A moment-to-moment analysis. *Journal of Consumer Research*, 31(3), 592–598.

Wühr, P., Lange, B. P., & Schwarz, S. (2017). Tears or fears? Comparing gender stereotypes about movie preferences to actual preferences. *Frontiers in Psychology*, 8, 428.

Wyer, R. S., & Collins, J. E. (1992). A theory of humor elicitation. *Psychological Review*, 99(4), 663.

Yip, J. A., & Martin, R. A. (2006). Sense of humor, emotional intelligence, and social competence. *Journal of Research in Personality*, 40(6), 1202–1208.

Yoon, H. J., & Kim, Y. (2014). The moderating role of gender identity in responses to comedic violence advertising. *Journal of Advertising*, 43(4), 382–396.

Yoon, I. (2016). Why is it not just a joke? Analysis of Internet memes associated with racism and hidden ideology of color blindness. *Journal of Cultural Research in Art Education*, 33.

Yovetich, N. A., Dale, J. A., & Hudak, M. A. (1990). Benefits of humor in reduction of threat-induced anxiety. *Psychological Reports*, 66(1), 51–58.

Yue, X. D., Hao, X., & Goldman, G. L. (2010). Humor styles, dispositional optimism, and mental health among undergraduates in Hong Kong and China. *Journal of Psychology in Chinese Societies*, 11(2), 173–188.

Yue, X. D., Jiang, F., Lu, S., & Hiranandani, N. (2016). To be or not to be humorous? Cross cultural perspectives on humor. *Frontiers in Psychology*, 7, 1495.

Yue, X. D., Liu, K. W. Y., Jiang, F., & Hiranandani, N. A. (2014). Humor styles, self-esteem, and subjective happiness. *Psychological Reports*, 115(2), 517–525.

Zeigler-Hill, V., McCabe, G. A., & Vrabel, J. K. (2016). The dark side of humor: DSM-5 pathological personality traits and humor styles. *Europe's Journal of Psychology*, 12(3), 363.

Zillmann, D., & Cantor, J. R. (1976). A disposition theory of humor and mirth. In A. J. Chapman & H. C. Foot (Eds.), *Humor and laughter: Theory, research and applications* (pp. 93–115). London: Transaction Publishers.

Ziv, A. (1984). *Personality and sense of humor*. New York: Springer.

Ziv, A. (1988). Teaching and learning with humor: Experiment and replication. *The Journal of Experimental Education*, 57(1), 4–15.

Ziv, A., Gorenstein, E., & Moris, A. (1986). Adolescents' evaluation of teachers using disparaging humour. *Educational Psychology*, 6(1), 37–44.

Zweyer, K., Velker, B., & Ruch, W. (2004). Do cheerfulness, exhilaration, and humor production moderate pain tolerance? A FACS study. *Humor*, 17(1–2), 85–119.

INDEX

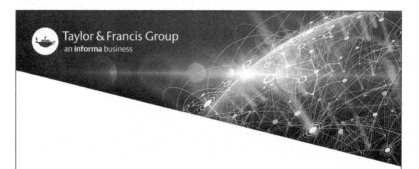